T0149693

HARNESS YOUR HERO

A TRANSFORMATIONAL 12-STAGE JOURNEY TO CREATE YOUR ULTIMATE YOU

ABBIE-LEA VERCO

BALBOA.PRESS

A DIVISION OF HAY HOUSE

Balboa Press books may be ordered through booksellers or by contacting:

Balboa Press
A Division of Hay House
1663 Liberty Drive
Bloomington, IN 47403
www.balboapress.com.au
1 (877) 407-4847

ISBN: 978-1-5043-2017-7 (sc)
ISBN: 978-1-5043-2020-7 (e)

Print information available on the last page.

Balboa Press rev. date: 01/07/2020

Dedicated to the men of my life:

my darling son, Braydon,

whose birth opened up a new Hero's Journey

for me to experience

and my beloved husband,

*who met me at the threshold and has joined me
in our adventure down our Yellow Brick Road.*

Dedicated to the men of my life:

my darling son, Braydon,

whose birth opened up a new Hero's Journey

for me to experience

and my beloved husband,

who met me at the threshold and has joined me
in our adventure down our Yellow Brick Road.

Contents

PREFACE

A Journey with a purpose

Getting the most out of your time working through this book

As you work through this book, I think you will agree that this is more than just an ordinary book. It is a guide; a formula for you to create your ideal roadmap and discover, go after, and create your ultimate life. After all, to MAP out your life is to create a **M**assive **A**ction **P**lan.

This book is divided into 12 sections, each broken into segments for you to ponder. I strongly urge you work through one section at a time so that you will have time to think about how to apply what you are learning and discovering to your life.

The great mission of our day is not conquering the sea or space, disease or tyranny. The grand quest which calls to the hero in every one of us is to become fully alive—to stand up and claim our birthright, which is inner freedom, love and radiant purpose. By fulfilling this, we transform the world.

Jacob Nordby

One reason most books don't transform us is that we are so eager to get to the next section; we don't pause and take the time to seriously consider what we have just learnt. We rush to the next truth without reflecting on the one we have just uncovered.

Don't just skim through these pages; interact with them. Take notes, send emails and ask for feedback—join our community and discuss what you are learning. Make it your own. Personalise it! The books that have helped me most are the ones that I have fully experienced, rather than just observed.

The energy that you put into this experience will mean you have either speculation or revelation: the power is in your hands.

Success is not just what you accomplish in your life;
it is about what you inspire others to do!

I am really proud of this book and the secrets that it holds within. The thing is, we don't want these gems to stay hidden secrets locked within the pages of this book. I think that these gems are so precious that I want to share them with you right now, so that you, too, can utilise their wisdom to unlock your true potential.

If you believe that today is the day for you to start your extraordinary journey and harness your hero, then turn the page and enter your very own Hero's Journey of possibility and adventure.

Grab a special notebook to become your 'playbook' or create a Word document or somewhere on your computer to keep your thoughts together so that your notes can become your personal blueprint for success.

INTRODUCTION

To structure or not to structure? That is the question...
Do you want to live your life by design or by default?

Every story has a beginning, a middle and an end. In the beginning, you look at where you are in your own story (journey), then you decide that something else needs to take shape and you make a decision for change. You make a change, a stand, a decision or form a resolve that may, at first, be a great source of conflict and takes you into a whole new and unfamiliar place. After facing many foes and overcoming various obstacles, if you are being true to yourself, you will become the victor and take home the prize.

If only creating the life you dream of was that easy.

The thing is, there are many forms of strategies and systems that we can subscribe to and we find many self-help books spouting about winning formulas. How do we know which one will work for us? Or do we believe those who say 'screw the system and the structures' and allow life to evolve organically and 'go with the flow'?

In the end, your story (your journey) should dictate the kind of structure you follow or whether you want to follow a structure at all. Let your character define your story and your story define your structure and then use a formula, if necessary, to tighten your personal manuscript/memoire/story. The trick is to initially let the ideas flow. This becomes your vision and, without that, the journey is a stagnant one of no interest that just leaves you reacting to the circumstances around you. Once you have your vision, the next stage is about focusing your story—making sure that the plot line (the journey) is one that you are enjoying and that is leading you closer to your desired destination.

Joseph Campbell researched and came up with 17 stages of what he called The Hero's Journey. These stages later got refined down to 12.

The 12 Stages of the Hero's Journey

Psychologist Carl Jung believed that behind the fabric of human existence there lies archetypes: 'Constantly repeating characters which occur in the dreams of all people and the myths of all cultures.' Jung concluded that these archetypes are a reflection of a common story (framework) that we all share.

These same thoughts and concepts were later picked up on by author, mythologist and lecturer Joseph Campbell, who wrote the book *The Hero with a Thousand Faces*. It was his opinion that there lies a structure behind every story—one shared story or myth that carries all the basics, and that story reflects each of our lives.

For some reason, these patterns of story are so common that they are recreated in all the epic movies and novels of our time. It could be concluded that this story framework reflects our everyday lives and journeys so much that we design it back into the stories we share.

Due to this phenomenon, we realise that it is most important to find yourself on The Hero's Journey; to start on the path of discovery of your true journey.

Where are you on your Hero's Journey?

The Hero's Journey begins…

*A hero is an ordinary individual who finds
the strength to persevere and endure
in spite of overwhelming obstacles.*

Christopher Reeve

*If you want to make the world a better place,
take a look at yourself, and make a change.*

Michael Jackson

Chapter 1:
The Ordinary World

For every goal, experience or time of change in an area of our lives, we begin in the mundane or ordinary world, where everything appears the status quo. Or is it? Everything seems okay, but what is okay? And how do we know when okay is actually not okay? Sometimes, a soft, small voice inside your head tells you that you are not happy and that life is not where you want it to be. You can't quite put your finger on it yet, but you just get this niggling feeling that there is more to life than where you are at.

This is where we live before we start our new journey. We are oblivious of the adventures to come. It is our safe place. Our everyday life where we learn crucial details about who we are, our true nature, capabilities and outlook on life. This anchors us as the human we are and makes it easier for us to understand and truly know who we are—our identity. Once we are clear on who we are and who we want to be, then and only then, can we truly start on our adventure to a better land.

The *Matrix's* Morpheus put it like this:

It's that feeling you have had all your life. That feeling that something was wrong with the world. You don't know what it is but it's there, like a splinter in your mind, driving you mad.

Where are you in your Hero's Journey right now? Are you happy with where you are? Do you feel that something's just not quite how you want it to be? That something needs to be changed? Is it something in your environment? Could it be that it is you who needs to make the change?

You feel it, don't you? That there should be something more. That there could be an alternate path that leads you to feel you have a more extraordinary life?

Harness Your Hero

Listen to the voice that separates you from your ordinary world, because it's asking you to take a risk on you. To step out in faith and follow your Hero's Journey. What does it say?

'As we think, so shall we be.' *As we think…* Not as we act or as we have more stuff or as we reach great successes, but as we think.

Our mind is a high-functioning hard drive. It continually receives information and we have programmed it to naturally filter and process that information even while we are sleeping.

'I have programmed my mind?' you might be thinking. Well, yes, we each program our minds consciously or subconsciously. So, it is important to understand how we do this, so that we can make sure we are putting the right software into our minds to run the 'programs' that will allow us the most success in our lives.

We receive information in a myriad of ways. We can take information in through what we see: visually. What we hear: auditorily. What we feel: kinaesthetically. What we smell: olfactorily. And what we taste: gustatorily.

Every second of every day, our body is experiencing things through our senses and transmitting those messages to our brain. Would you believe (fasten your seatbelts) that studies have shown that the brain takes in 200 million pieces of information EVERY SECOND! Now, I don't know about you, but I know that I can't consciously process 200 million bits of information a second; I would be a Looney Tune.

Thankfully, our brains are very smart pieces of machinery that are created to look after us, so although we receive all this information, we only process a small proportion of it; seven (plus or minus two) bits or 'chunks' of information.

This is where our 'programming' comes into it. At the point where all this information is streaming in through our senses into our bodies, we filter through it and only take in what we tell it to.

So, let's look at this a little further. I would like to do a little demonstration with you. I would like you to bring this book up close to your face to shut out everything else in the room. Then, I want you, without looking, to think of all the things in the room that are blue. Once you believe you have counted in your head, without looking, everything that is blue, then I want you to lower the book and see how you did. Were there more blue things in the room than you counted (deleted)? Did you count a larger number of things than was actually there (distort)? Or did you just take a bit of a guess (generalise)? Interesting, isn't it? Are you suddenly noticing blue things that you have never seen before?

We set up these filters by telling our brains what we want to see. If you now take a good, hard look around at everything that is blue and then close your eyes, I am sure that you would remember everything that is blue in the room. But if I asked you, when you opened your eyes, what in the room was red, you probably wouldn't do so well as your brain was looking for blue things, not for red.

Our mind is deleting information all the time as one of its natural roles. That is the reason we might go into a crowded party and not be able to hear anything and then once we get into a conversation with someone, all the other noises are soon drowned out and, if we are engrossed in the conversation, we will get to a point where we won't even hear the other noises. We take in what we focus on and filter out the rest. We filter information by deleting it, as demonstrated above, distorting it or generalising it.

I recall going on a school camp to a place called Storey's Creek. It was out in the country with old dorm rooms and lots of open space. A very picturesque setting that gave the feeling that you had gone back in time about a hundred years.

Harness Your Hero

On the second night of camp, our group sat around a campfire telling ghost stories until our teachers told us it was time to retire for the evening. So, we snuggled up into our sleeping bags on the bunk beds. The beds moved and squeaked and the wind rustled through the roof, and the room that had seemed so warm and inviting through the day had certainly somehow taken on an eerie and chilled feel. One of the more timid young lasses would let out a little squeal each time the tin roof rattled a little, and that night seemed to go on for the longest time.

Now, the dorm room had not changed, and they were the same noises that we had heard and ignored through the day, but we had distorted the information that our ears were delivering to us due to the stories that we had been telling.

On the bus ride home, then, I found it interesting that we were having a conversation about dorm-style accommodation and many of the students stated that 'all' dorm rooms were eerie and creepy. *All* dorm rooms? Had they been in *all* dorm rooms? Could it possibly be that every dorm room on planet Earth was eerie and creepy? Possibly not, but our minds can easily clump things together and make generalisations.

So, how do we come up with the conclusions that we do? Well, that is due to the filters that we sift the information through.

We have seven filters that we sift all information through.

1. Your environment (time, space, matter and energy).

2. Language (the words we use).

3. Memories.

4. Decisions.

5. Meta-Programs—Mental shortcuts that direct your decisions, behaviours, actions and interactions with others. They are internal representations of your external experience of reality. They determine how your brain pays attention to things and what it pays attention to. For instance, whether you are motivated away from pain or towards pleasure.

6. Attitudes.

7. Values and beliefs.

The fact of the matter is, how we feel about our lives and where we are at is determined by these filters. If this is the case and we want to change our lives, we need to evaluate these filters.

Remember, 'if you always do what you have always done, you will always get what you have always got.'

We will explore filters later in this book, but let's get started on our personal journey with a bit of an assessment of where things are at currently. To know where we are on our journey, it can be useful to do a quick evaluation of where our life is at.

Welcome to your Wheel of Life!

The Wheel of Life is a great exercise and tool for helping you create more balance and success in your life. It is often used in coaching and is a great foundation exercise when goal-setting.

As a starting point for creating balance, happiness and success in your life, the Wheel of Life is the ideal tool to kickstart your journey. Using this tool, you will be able to reflect and gain some insight into the balance of your life and how satisfied you are in key areas. Following on from this self-reflection, you can utilise this exercise to go deeper into the rabbit hole of why your Wheel of Life looks the way it does, what you would like your Wheel to look like, and start to look at what small changes can be made to bring about the best results.

Essentially, the Wheel of Life is divided into different areas or categories that are important to you. There is a scoring system behind using the Wheel, where you simply reflect and rate your satisfaction levels out of ten, where one is closest to the centre of the circle and ten is at the edge of the circle.

You will find that you will be able to score yourself in the majority of key areas in your life. However, before you rush into it and complete the Wheel, you may like to think about whether there are any other categories or specific areas you would like to get an understanding of, such as 'Spirituality' or 'Contribution to Society'. Perhaps you may want to have 'Family and Friends' as two separate categories to understand each more specifically. So, here is our template; feel free to use this or draw up your own. Note that the categories on the Wheel are suggestions only.

ACTION STEPS

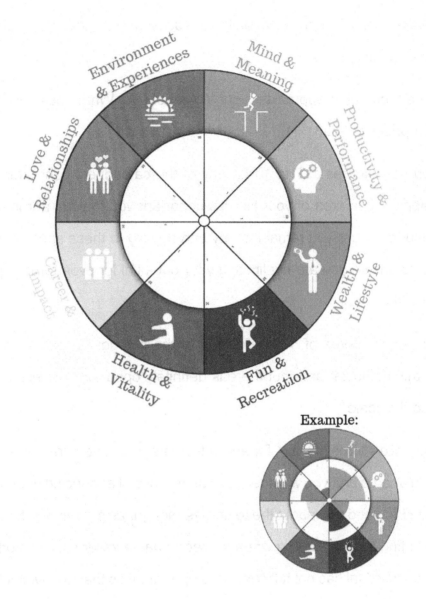

Example:

Remember, this is about you finding happiness and balance in your life, so it will need to be clear and simple for you to understand.

One of the biggest benefits of the Wheel of Life is the pictorial representation it gives of your satisfaction with life.

When your wheel is completed, it will give you a spider-like diagram or 'inner-circle' of your satisfaction levels and allow you to quickly and easily identify any gaps

Harness Your Hero

between where you are now and where you desire to be. I recommend drawing this up in your playbook to keep your thoughts together.

Now that you understand the building blocks of the wheel, let's go ahead and actually complete it!

Take a moment to appreciate your Wheel of Life. What does it look like? Are there any surprises to you?

If you have scores of 7 to 10 for any of the categories, congratulations! You are very happy in this area of your life. It's important you maintain or improve what you are doing to ensure you remain happy and healthy in these specific areas. This is important to ensure you are not limiting your potential for even further growth and satisfaction in this area.

If you have scores of 5 to 7 for any of the categories, you are reasonably satisfied in this particular area but there is definitely opportunity to explore ideas to move this up the scale.

If you have scores of 0 to 4 for any of the categories, you are not very satisfied in this particular area and you will need to explore ways of enhancing your satisfaction here. No need to get down about these scores though, as scores of 0 to 4 are full of opportunity! I find it quite exciting when someone has a lower score as often it's the case that the individual has not fully explored opportunities that are available to them. It's also the area where the individual can grow the most and get the most value!

I encourage you to answer the below questions:

1. Why did you score yourself in each category the way you did?

2. What is my ideal score for each category to achieve in the next month, three months, six months, one year?

3. Where are my biggest gaps in satisfaction levels?

4. Which area of my life do I primarily want to focus on to enhance my satisfaction levels?

An important thing to remember is that this is *your* Wheel of Life. Is your current wheel crooked or is it balanced?

What happens when you try to move forward and you have a crooked wheel? How efficient and effective are you going to be in life if you cannot move forward in a balanced way?

It is very easy to become extremely satisfied in one area, but at what cost?

For example, you can spend all your time and energy working on your career and make some fantastic progress. Perhaps you will even become extremely satisfied with your finances and wealth. However, what may happen to your relationships? Your health and wellbeing? Are you having fun along the way?

The key is to find the balance and that is the beauty of the wheel. To do this, you want to grow your wheel, not balance your wheel by trading off in some areas of your life. It's about moving forward, challenging yourself and pushing your boundaries to expand your wheel and make it bigger while maintaining a balance.

NOW LET'S TAKE SOME ACTION!

Now it is time to put this wheel into motion.

You now have a visual snapshot of how satisfied you are in different areas of your life. Through reflection, you have now identified the biggest gaps between where you are now and where you would like to be.

Commit yourself to taking action TODAY. What are the specific actions or steps

Harness Your Hero

that you are going to take to enhance your satisfaction in your desired area? Write what you will do down on the same piece of paper that your wheel is on. Keep your wheel close by in a place that you can easily refer to on a daily basis.

Track your progress! The wheel provides a snapshot in time of your satisfaction levels and, ultimately, happiness. Complete the wheel on a regular basis so you can easily track your progress. I recommend at least once every six months, depending on what your goals are and when you have aimed to achieve them.

You might like to write in your book here or add this to your playbook you have created.

'Bloom where you are planted!'

Review and Goals

Love and Relationships

Environment and Experiences

Mind and Meaning

Productivity and Performance

Wealth and Lifestyle

Fun and Recreation

Health & Vitality

Career and Impact

My Mission

Rewards and Celebrations

Have You Checked Your Life Priorities Lately?

Your life's priorities are whatever you spend time doing.

Think about what things you do on any given day. What are you doing with your time, money and energy? Guess what? Where you put your time and money indicates what your current priorities are.

Most of us never even think about what we spend our time doing. We get up, we go to our place of study and/or work, we come home at the end of the day. The story it tells us when we break this down is a very clearly defined set of priorities.

So, if you come home at night and flop down on the couch and watch TV until you go to bed, those five hours or so you just spent watching TV means that this is one of your life priorities.

If you spent eight hours working at a job you hate, that job is still your priority. If this works for you, then you're doing okay. But if you spend time wishing you had a more fulfilling job or even something as simple as more time to read or learn to paint, then it's time to think about your life priorities.

Think about why you're doing something. Think about all the things you spend your time doing on an average day or even on the weekend. Why do you do those things? Are they really life priorities or do you just do them because that's what you've always done?

Think about why you do that mindless thing you do every day, whether it's going on Facebook, watching YouTube videos, or just random internet searching. Is it because you're tired or because you've gotten yourself in a rut without even realising it? Is there something you could be doing that would make you happier?

Think about how you're going about things. Is there a better way of doing the things you've decided are life priorities? For example, do you find that your entire weekend is spent running errands, cleaning and cooking? Buying groceries has to be done so that you don't go hungry, but are there better ways of accomplishing that chore?

For example:

Could you get the groceries during the week on the way home from work? Could you go after dinner one night when the stores are probably less crowded and it would be faster to get done anyway? Is there a grocery store near where you work? Could you get groceries on your lunch hour? Could you order them online and have them delivered or pick them up on your way home?

By thinking of more efficient ways to do things, you've just suddenly freed up your valuable time. By getting groceries during the week, you've just given yourself more time on the weekend to do something you want to do and all you've done is change how you accomplish one of your other life priorities.

It's all about paying attention to what you do with your time and thinking about if there are better ways to accomplish the same task.

Are there things you want to do? Would you like to have more time just for you or to spend with your kids? To just read a book or go for a walk? It's important to take the time to consider what things you want to do or see or accomplish in your life.

It's easy to get caught up in the rush just to accomplish all your daily life activities and not really consider what you want to do or have in your life. Or worse yet, think that you'll do it 'someday'.

Once you know what you want, then you can take the steps to achieve it. So the next section of this book is about focusing on just that: your priorities.

PRIORITY 'ROCKS'

PICTURE THIS:

A trainer is addressing her class. She fills a jug with big rocks and asks the class if it's full.

The class responds with a 'yes'.

'Really? Let's see,' she says and proceeds to further add pebbles to the jug and again asks if the jug is full. The class responds and indicates that the jug is now full. The trainer again says, 'Really? Let's see.' The trainer then pours sand into the jug.

The trainer goes on to explain that the sand and the pebbles represent the small daily tasks we fill our lives with. If we don't fit our big rocks in first, our lives will fill with only sand and pebbles. BUT if we start with our big rocks, we create room for what's important in life—and the sand and pebbles can only fill the spaces in between.

pebbles

sands

rocks

Harness Your Hero

1. Think about where you are currently spending most of your time.

    1. _____

    2. _____

    3. _____

2. What is the **LARGEST thing(s) that DRAINS** your time at the moment?

_____

_____

_____

_____

3. What changes are you going to make in regard to this?

_____

_____

_____

_____

Now let's get really clear...

What are your Top 3 Priorities in life?

    1. _____
    2. _____
    3. _____

4. What one thing is MOST IMPORTANT to you right now?

_____

YOUR PERSONAL PRIORITY MANAGEMENT TOOL

Time to Reflect:

What changes will you make following what you have learned about yourself?

1. How does where you currently spend your time compare to your 'Priority Rocks'— your REAL priorities?

_____
_____
_____

2. What does this tell you?

_____
_____
_____

What Needs to Change?

3. What could you be doing differently?

_____
_____
_____

4. What is the SIMPLEST change/s you could make to prioritise your time better?	5. What are you PREPARED to change to prioritise your time better?	6. Smash those hurdles: what could get in the way? If you were going to sabotage yourself, how would you do it?
_____ _____ _____	_____ _____ _____	_____ _____ _____

So, the question really is, what will you commit to?

7. What WILL you change or do differently? Take a look at the entire worksheet and identify three actions you will take to focus on your PRIORITY ROCKS in life:

1st Action _____

By when _____

2nd Action _____

By when _____

3rd Action _____

By when _____

Put these actions all over the place, everywhere you will see them.
Have them as a screensaver, on the bathroom mirror, on the fridge
and in your wallet. Set reminders on your phone to prompt you.

This is a contract you are entering into with yourself. Do yourself proud.

"I am committed to achieving these three actions!"

Signed: _____ **Date:** _____

Self-Reflection Questions

- What have you learnt about yourself from thinking about where you are currently at and where you would like to be?

- What are the most important things in your life?

- What does your ideal day look like?

- Are you where you want to be?

- Are you ready for change?

- What is the 'more' for you?

We must be willing to let go of the life we planned so as to have the life that is waiting for us.

Joseph Campbell

Chapter 2:
The Call to Adventure

In the last chapter, we wrote about the Ordinary World. We wrote about the niggling feeling that something might just not be where you would like it to be. You may realise on reflecting that there is something that you feel, have heard or have seen that you would like in your world.

The purpose of the Call to Adventure is to wake the 'hero' up. It reveals that there's something else outside of the Ordinary World. The 'call' can come in many different shapes and sizes. Let's look at some of the epic stories. The call in *Lord of the Rings* came in the form of Frodo's ring. In the *Wizard of Oz*, it was Dorothy's tornado.

Back in the real world, the call is opportunity knocking. It might be a job advertisement or a chance to take up a new hobby. It could be a health scare that leads you on a health and wellness journey or some neighbours moving in that is the start of a new friendship. These are just a few examples of signs that point to an opportunity for change. And, thus, for growth.

It is important to remember that the call to adventure is a *choice*.

As with anything heroic, there must be action. The hero needs to choose to accept the call before moving on with the story.

Our adventure begins when we receive a call to action and take it up. This Call to Adventure could be a massive life-changing moment or it could be a simple phone call or conversation but, whatever the call is, and however it appears, it ultimately disrupts the comfort of our Ordinary World and presents a challenge or quest that must be undertaken.

For us to hear the Call to Adventure, we often come face to face with one of two things:

- **Pain**: Something in our world that has gotten too hard to ignore or to put up with—something that will give us the push to move out of our ordinary world.

- **Pleasure**: The desire to gain something that we want—something that will push you further along your Hero's Journey.

What is it you're no longer willing to accept as it is anymore? What is a new outcome that you want to achieve for yourself: a goal enticing and powerful enough that would make you want to leave behind the old and step into the new? That's the elixir you are after! That becomes your Call to Adventure.

Now that you are hearing the Call to Adventure, you may discover that it is not the first time you have heard this call. In the Hero's Journey, many heroes, at first, actually refuse the call.

They might not think that they have the tools for the job, be reluctant to step up, be fearful of the challenge or perhaps just don't think that the mission is right for them or aligned with their desired outcomes.

The only way we truly know if the Call to Adventure is for us, is to follow it and see where it leads.

Marianne Williamson said:

Our deepest fear is not that we are inadequate. Our deepest fear is that we are powerful beyond measure. It is our light, not our darkness, that most frightens us. We ask ourselves, who am I to be brilliant, gorgeous, talented, fabulous? Actually, who are you not to be? You are a child of God. Your playing small, doesn't serve the world. There's nothing enlightened about shrinking so that other people won't feel insecure around you. We are all meant to shine, as children do. We were born to make manifest the glory of God that is within us. It's not just in some of us; it's in everyone. And as we let our own light shine, we unconsciously give other people permission to do the same. As we're liberated from our own fear, our presence automatically liberates others.

I once heard someone say that you are either green and growing or red and rotting. We never stay the same. For heroes who refuse the call to adventure, there's only one thing that happens: they start rotting. They start dying inside, until, one day, the call grabs their attention and they have no choice but to answer it.

Whatever stage of your journey you are in, what is calling to you to step up and be different or do something differently to take life to the next level? Is there enough pain in your world for you to take a stand and change that area or, in fact, is it a goal or something that you are wanting that can drive you to move forward? Do you know what the elixir is that you seek? Where might your new adventure begin?

When I was in my early 20s, I knew there were two things that I loved: I loved being able to learn and pass on that knowledge, and I knew I loved being creative and exploring the potential of the human mind.

There were so many things that I wanted to do and try, but straight after high school, I didn't really try very much at all. I worked average jobs and studied the 'safe' educational options, as I didn't believe I could do any more than that.

One day, I was driving down into the City and the new sign was just being put up for the Inveresk Campus of the University of Tasmania. It was their performing arts campus.

I don't know what it was on that day that led me to drive down the winding driveway to the new campus, as I hadn't even done drama as a subject at high school.

I stood out the front of the university and, for the first time, really contemplated how life could look different for me.

This Call to Adventure saw me completing a Bachelor of Contemporary Arts Degree, which saw me starting my own events company and then going on to study teaching, which led to coaching, and a whole different world started opening up for me. I achieved things beyond my wildest dreams and opened up to the reality that anything is possible.

How about you? What opportunity is offering itself up to you right now?

We have now explored our Wheel of Life and how satisfied we are in these areas and we have looked at our priorities. The one thing to then take into consideration and add to the mix is a really important ingredient: it is knowing and working with your values.

Let's break down what we mean by *values* and two other words closely associated.

Values are a set of underlying principles and qualities that we use to decide what is and isn't important in our life.

Principles: these are what we base decisions on, e.g. having good family relationships, being honest, having purpose, being creative, etc.

Qualities: this is how we would like others to see us, e.g. confident, a leader, empathic, committed, etc.

Before we can set a goal for our life, it helps to understand our values. Everyone has a different set of values, and ways in which the values can be achieved and/or demonstrated. Both values and the way we carry out values can shift and alter over time.

Think of your values like a compass, if you will. The compass points you in the right direction. Your goals and actions are the specific path to follow to get there.

I really like the river metaphor to help describe this.

The direction of the river represents our values.

Provided that our river is heading in the direction of our values, life can still be fulfilling. The specific course we take is shaped by all those things that life throws our way—and so some of us may meander down a creek bed, while others may meet a larger stream and be influenced by other people, before returning to the main riverbed and the original direction we had chosen.

There are many things that can influence the direction we take in life. For me, I found chronic physical pain to be one of those influences. It can mean different functional abilities, changed roles, leaving a job and needing to spend time with health- care providers.

This can, without you meaning it to, get in the way of living a life that is still moving towards things we value. Some values we hold conflict with trying to reduce pain, while others become more or less important because of the way pain affects life (this could be physical, mental, spiritual or emotional pain).

To live well despite the challenges you are facing (having chronic pain, financial issues, etc.), having goals that are in line with your values is vital. We don't often think about what is important and why it is so important!

ACTION STEPS

An exercise to identify your values

In this exercise, we're going to decide which values are very important to you. Below is a list of values to get you started. To help you think about what you would do with your life if I could wave a magic wand and all the pain, all the thoughts and feelings and memories you have about your pain would no longer have any impact on you. What would you do with your life? What would you start, stop, do more of, or less of? How would you behave differently? What would show the world that this magic had happened?

Martin Seligman came up with the VIA (Values in Action) Survey
that you can complete free online and this might help you.
https://www.viacharacter.org/www/Character-Strengths-Survey

Don't be limited by this list. These are just some suggestions!

Affectionate	Joyful
Ambitious	Kind
Appreciative	Leader
Brave	Logical
Calm	Loving
Caring	Loyal
Cheerful	Having manners
Committed	Maturity
Compassionate	Patient
Concerned	Patriotic
Confident	Peaceful
Conscientious	Perseverance
Considerate	Persistence
Contented	Persuasiveness
Cooperative	Pleasant
Courageous	Polite
Decisiveness	Positive
Dependability	Rational
Determination	Reliable
Diligence	Religious
Discernment	Resourceful
Encouraging	Respect
Enthusiastic	Responsible
Fairness	Security
Faithfulness	Self-confident
Flexibility	Self-control
Forgiveness	Sensitive
Generosity	Sincerity
Gentleness	Successful
Giving	Tactful
Gratitude	Thankful
Happiness	Thorough
Helpfulness	Thrifty
Honest	Tolerant
Humble	Truthful
Humorous	Unselfish
Impartial	Versatile
Imaginative	Warm-hearted
Intelligent	Witty

Harness Your Hero

My top five values and descriptive statements

Value	Descriptive Personal Statement

Examples:

Calm   I remain calm even during difficult times

Family   I honour and support my family to the best of my ability

How to make choices about goals and actions based on values

When you have an opportunity in your life to make a choice about a goal or action, it can be difficult to decide what to do. Before you make a decision, review your top three values, then ask yourself:

Does this decision honour my value of _____? (#1 value)

Does this decision honour my value of_____? (#2 value)

Does this decision honour my value of_____? (#3 value)

If the answer is 'No', then you will most probably not be happy in the long-term choosing this goal or action.

What is the one thing I could do right now, today, to live more in alignment with my values?

_____

Don't be afraid to revisit your values as you feel you need to.

Now, think about your values and priorities and what parts of your Wheel of Life you wanted to work on. Start by focusing on one area.

HOME RUN ...

The Area of Life I'm going to zoom in on below is

_____

1. List the <u>short-term goals</u> (i.e. ones relating to the next few weeks and months) you wish to achieve and take action on.

    1)

    2)

    3)

2. <u>Describe in detail HOW you will achieve</u> these same short-term goals.

    What ACTIONS will you need to take?

    1)

    2)

    3)

3. What is the <u>timeframe for achieving</u> these actions?

    1)

    2)

    3)

4. <u>What support will you need, and who can you go to</u>, to help make these short-term goals become a reality?

    1)

    2)

    3)

5. <u>What personal changes need to happen</u> in order to bring these short-term goals into reality?

(Changes could be around lifestyle choices such as sleep and food, behaviour, attitude, choices, people you associate with.)

1)

2)

3)

LAST OF ALL ...

Now let's look at the next level – the long-term.

It's important to keep your 'eye-on-the-prize' and the 'big picture'.

With the _____ **Area**

of Life in mind, think about the long-term (over the next few years).

6. List the <u>long-term goals</u> (i.e. over the next few years) you wish to achieve and take action on.

1)

2)

3)

7. <u>Describe in detail HOW you will achieve</u> these same long-term goals.

What ACTIONS will you need to take?

1)

2)

3)

8. What is the approximate <u>timeframe for achieving</u> these actions? What year will it be? How old will you be?

   1)

   2)

9. What support will you need, and who can you go to, to help make these long-term goals become a reality?

   1)

   2)

   3)

10. What personal changes need to happen in order to bring these long-term goals into reality?

    (Changes could be around lifestyle choices such as sleep and food, behaviour, attitude, choices, people you associate with.)

    1)

    2)

    3)

Harness Your Hero

Self-Reflection Questions

- What do you value?

- What are your priorities?

- What is the treasure you are after?

- What is your life's vision?

- What goals do you have?

- How recently have you reviewed them?

*Life opens up opportunities to you,
and you either take them
or you stay afraid of taking them.*

Jim Carrey

Chapter 3:
The Refusal of the Call

Very often, the call is refused. It could be through inaction (a failure to seize the opportunity) or it could be flat-out refusal ('I'm not going to do it'). We can often put blocks in the way of accepting the call. We might tell ourselves that we are not ready, or that we are not sure which path we want to follow.

In *Star Wars*, Luke initially turns down the opportunity to fly off his planet with Obi Wan. He didn't want to leave his aunt and uncle, who needed him. Han Solo also initially refuses an opportunity to stay and help the Rebellion. He was motivated by dollars and staying on the safe side of things.

In 2001, when I received the call to teach drama to high school students, a friend of mine decided to come and give a hand as well. This new adventure and the opportunity to work with teenagers really excited us both. After having worked with the young people for six months, the principal said that if we were to complete a two-year Bachelor of Teaching, we would be able to work full-time at the school as English-Drama teachers. I decided that, even though it would be a lot of work to study and work and raise a young child, the payoff would be worth it and I signed up to start my next degree. My friend decided that she did not think it was a good idea and she went back to working at the pizza bar that she had been working at previously. My new journey started, and hers finished as quickly as it was about to start.

In short, refusing the call ends the story. There is nothing more—you stay in the ordinary world and nothing changes.

If you want change, then you must accept the call.

Thankfully, we don't always get just one chance. Let's go back to our earlier example of Luke. His initial refusal is reversed when the reasons for his refusal are removed (by some enthusiastic Stormtroopers). When we're tempted to refuse a call, identifying the reasons can help. Once we know what's keeping us from the adventure, we can remove the obstacle or at least reduce its effects.

Fear is the great motivator.

Behind every reason for staying where we are, is fear. Fear comes in many shapes and sizes. We might think we're not good enough or we might fail. We might not want to leave what has become our comfort zone. We may have been taught that 'this is the way it is—just accept it'. That's all fear.

The greatest enemy of fear is a mirror. Stare down your fears. Look fear in the face and see it for what it is: False Evidence Appearing Real. When we look at what we fear, there is always an element of truth in the fear; however, the greatest and strongest lies always have an element of truth surrounded by a much bigger element of a lie. I find when I stop and calmly work out which part is the lie and which smaller part is the truth, I am able to overcome the fear because I can put it into perspective. It's always when our perspective is out of order that the fear is able to take hold of us.

When a great adventure is offered, you don't refuse it.

Amelia Earhart

You should always be ready and on the lookout for a Call to Adventure. If you aren't aware of the opportunity, you can't answer the call. It is also worth taking note to make sure you have resolved any issues in the Ordinary World, as it can have a strong pull on keeping you where you are.

ACTION STEPS

What is the call that you have been refusing?

Become curious about the call and write down what the Calls to Adventure are in your world at the moment. Are you thinking about starting a new job? A new hobby? Getting a new health routine? Moving home? Getting a pet? Anything and everything that you want to do—write it down.

Now I want you to write down all of the reasons that you don't think you can have or do that goal at the moment. Once you have looked at that, I want you to look at how you can turn those challenges into actionable goals that can move you towards where you want to be.

For example:

When my business partner and I decided to start a coaching and training business, we set to task to write our very first funding proposal. We had done our research and had crunched the numbers and we needed funding of $150,000.

Neither of us had written a proposal for anything like this amount of money and, quite frankly, we didn't know whether we had what it took and, in fact, we put off writing that proposal for three months!

In that time, we spoke to so many people who told us that what we were proposing (a program for at-risk students to help them re-engage with their education) was really needed and we should to take the plunge. As the vision grew for us, we knew we had to stop giving in to the fear and jump in, feet and all.

The result: we applied for the funding and were granted the full amount and, just four weeks later, started changing the lives of 100 young people.

We haven't stopped working with people to transform their lives since. It was a game-changer that turned the directions of our lives. It was also when working on that program that my business partner and I decided we wanted to be more than business partners and, as history has it, we are now married. How different things may have been if we had not taken that plunge.

ACTION STEPS

If we don't align our beliefs with what we want in life, we will continue to create the life we currently have. You see, whether we know it or not, we create situations that uphold our beliefs.

I would like you to think about the area of your life that you are currently choosing to focus on. Now take out your workbook and write down all the reasons why you're not getting what you want. For example: *I don't have the time. I don't have the money. I'm too tired, I am not good enough.* Now look at your list. These are limiting beliefs. As long as you believe them to be true, they will remain true for you, and you will experience life according to those beliefs.

I know (as this was true for me when I first did this action step) that some of you may already be struggling with the above paragraph. You may even be coming up with reasons to justify why you hold the beliefs you do. If you are one of these people, I ask that, just for now, you suspend your judgement. Agree only to the fact that, even if your beliefs are true, this does not mean that things can't change. This book is about change, and, when you began reading it, you made a commitment to yourself to let change happen.

Now I would like you to look at the limiting beliefs that you have written down and write a new empowering belief to replace it.

For instance, I was holding on to a limiting belief that I was not good enough. I wasn't aware of this, but when I wrote down that I wanted a loving and supporting relationship, and then I looked at why I didn't have it, I had a lot of statements about not being pretty enough, not being smart enough or classy enough to attract the type of partner I so longed for. After looking at these as limiting beliefs, I replaced them with: *I am smart and healthy and ready for love.* Twelve months later (okay, not saying it happened overnight), I found my perfect man and I am enjoying a relationship better than I ever knew could possibly exist.

Now when you interrupt your limiting belief patter, replace it with this new one. The more you say it and think it, the quicker it will be embedded in your mind and become your automatic go-to belief.

Self-Reflection Questions

- Are you allowing fear to stop you from answering the Call to Adventure?

- What is the adventure out there for you?

- Will you embrace it?

- What motivates you to leave your 'story' and start your adventure?

A mentor enables a person to achieve.
A hero shows what achievement looks like.

John C. Mather

Chapter 4:
Meeting the Mentor

Once we decide to take action in our lives, it can be amazing the changes that start happening. When we really commit to moving forward, we tend to find that a mentor will arise. A person (or it could even be a book or YouTube channel to start with) will come into your world to support you in moving forward.

Once we start taking action, good things happen. Don't get me wrong—it doesn't mean it is all beers and skittles from here—but we attract good things to us. Action invites good energy our way. It's simple. Haven't you heard someone tell you about their goals and dreams in a very ho-hum kind of way? When it's obvious they're not committed, do you feel inspired?

But what happens when you listen to someone describe their dreams with total conviction? You feel like supporting them, right? You get caught up by their drive and even inspired. Once you start thinking about their dream, you think of someone they could talk to who has knowledge on their dream, a book they could read, or a company they could approach. Ideas start coming and then flow.

In the words of Goethe:

Until one is committed, there is hesitancy, the chance to draw back, always ineffectiveness. Concerning all acts of initiative and creation, there is one elementary truth the ignorance of which kills countless ideas and splendid plans: that the moment one definitely commits oneself, then providence moves too. All sorts of things occur to help one that would never otherwise have occurred. A whole stream of events issues from the decision, raising in one's favour all manner of unforeseen incidents, meetings and material assistance which no man could have dreamed would have come

his way. Whatever you can do or dream you can, begin it. Boldness
has genius, power and magic in it. Begin it now.

A wise mentor might appear in the form of a person, a book, a movie, or even the lyrics of a song. This special mentor might appear to give you a special tool or technique, advice, or training to help you face the challenges you will experience in your Hero's Journey.

As you focus on the elixir you're after in this journey, what or who could be your mentor(s)? With the internet at our fingertips, we're surrounded by an overflowing selection of mentors, either people you can meet in person, talk to over the phone, via the internet, or books, magazines, videos and audio programs from experts you haven't even met, from halfway across the world, who can give you 'real-time' advice.

Meeting the Wise Mentor

As you go about your day, keep your senses tuned in. Notice which mentors 'magically' come onto your radar to give you the much-needed support and advice you can use.

Is it going to be someone you meet buying coffee? A song on the radio on the way to work? A book you glance over? A program friends were discussing over lunch?

It is a good investment to always be on the lookout for wise mentors to support us along our Hero's Journey. What might you learn from them today?

*Seek out a personal coach
or mentor in the workplace.
He/she should push you when you need it
by encouraging and motivating you.
Don't be afraid of their honesty.*

Cathy Engelbert

ACTION STEPS

		The Books, DVDs, Internet Material, Magazines and/ or Audio I want to Read, Watch or Listen to:		
Author or Creator	Title	Advice or learning you want to gain or have gained	✓ When Done

Courses, Workshops or Programs I would like to do:			
Who is Delivering?	Title	Advice or learning you want to gain or have gained	✓ When Done

Harness Your Hero

*Turn Your Itty Bitty Pity Committee
into a strong board of directors....*

Who are the five people closest to you?

*Is this serving you? Do you need to
refocus who you are spending time with?*

*Who do you know that is successful
in the area you are focused on
improving? How can you tap into
their knowledge/time, etc.?*

Who are you going to champion?

*The best way to put something
into practice is to teach it to
someone else and pass it on.*

Self-Reflection Questions

- What movie, story, poem, artwork, concert or person has recently touched you?

- Whose message has warmed your heart; whose example has inspired you?

- How can you add these 'mentors' to your board of directors? (The directors on your board are the voices that you listen to in your mind when you are making decisions.)

- What confrontation/communication skills do you need for what's coming next?

I always wonder why birds stay in the same place when they can fly anywhere on the earth. Then I ask myself the same question.

Harun Yahya

Chapter 5:
Crossing the Threshold

Let's Recap:

- You've committed to making change and accepting the Call to Adventure.

- You have stepped into your very own Hero's Journey. As you move further into your journey, you will be exposed to a lot of new things; some good, some not. All of them will support your growth and your journey.

- Sometimes you might feel that you don't have what you need, and feel uncomfortable and out of your element. I am sure there will be times when you ask yourself if you should have left your ordinary world behind. We have all had these experiences. We call it 'growing pains' for a reason. As we stretch ourselves, we will feel the pains of the stretching, and then we will feel all that the new world has to offer us. There is a book titled *Feel the Fear and Do It Anyway.* This is where the Crossing of the Threshold comes into play.

Let's break down the definition of Crossing the Threshold:

Crossing – *A place where two roads meet OR the action of moving across or over something.*

Synonyms – *Passage, intersection, transit, crossroads, pass, cut through, intertwine.*

Threshold – *Opening; beginning.*

Synonyms – *Boundary, point of departure, starting point, dawn, door, verge, brink, entrance.*

Harness Your Hero

So, by definition, the crossing of the threshold is to move into a new beginning; enter a new door and start a different experience.

Let's look at how this stage of the journey works. Once the hero (insert your name here) has accepted the call, they have to cross from their old world over into the new. This crossing is made at the threshold. If there was anxiety at the Call to Adventure, the threshold can be downright terrifying. Saying goodbye to everything as you know it is not for the faint-hearted!

I don't know about you, but I am a *Lord of the Rings* fan.

If I take one more step, it will be the farthest away from home I've ever been.

When Sam follows Frodo on his adventure and takes that 'one more step', he leaves the familiar Shire behind him. He takes the same step that Dorothy (*Wizard of Oz*) took when she left Kansas, and Luke (*Star Wars*) took when he flew off in the Millennium Falcon.

These soon-to-be heroes all take a step into the unknown. However, they are not alone. For better or worse.

The crossing of thresholds is a highly symbolic act. It indicates commitment and change, leaving behind the old and accepting the new.

Threshold Guardians

At every 'gate' (new world, stage of life or beginning) there are the gatekeepers. The gatekeepers are called the 'Threshold Guardians' and their role is to make sure the hero is ready for the adventure to come. The Guardian may be an adversary, a neutral bystander, or a potential ally. They may help with advice, or try to test your readiness. Their goal may be to stop you from entering altogether.

If we go back for a moment to the Lord of the Rings, Sam first encounters the dark riders in the woods on the edge of the Shire and then he and his companions meet Strider at the Prancing Pony. The Nazgûl demonstrate the dangers of what's to come, while the ranger reinforces this message in the role of protector.

The Threshold Guardians can be pretty full-on sometimes.

In *Spiderman*, Peter Parker's threshold is guarded by a robber and his uncle. Peter chose to use his new powers selfishly at first; he was thinking about how to get money so he could buy a car and impress a girl! Not really the motivations of a hero, one might say. The robber highlighted Peter's self-interest, as he lets him go. His Uncle Ben's wise words as he was dying, 'With great power, comes great responsibility,' directs Peter back in the right direction.

When we decided to cross the threshold of running our own business, we met a few guardians. Barbara, Tim and Emma were three such guardians and they were working for different government departments that we were requesting funding and partnership through, and they helped Nathan and me navigate and learn the law (and lore) of this new world we were stepping into. Separately to this, there was an issue with intellectual property that needed to be sorted out, and that and funding issues introduced us to some of the harsh realities of running a training and coaching business. Sticking to our guns, we sorted out both the IP issues, legally, and worked through the payment of our program funds. These Threshold Guardians—some allies and some adversaries—taught us more than any college or book could have taught us about running our business. We learnt, and even won awards for the programs we were running at that time.

The Threshold Guardians, while not always adversaries, have to be dealt with. You need to pay attention to their advice, avoid their diversions, or solve the problem they represent. Above all, acknowledge them.

When I stop and think about whether I am up for the task of crossing the threshold, I think of how a diamond is created. Diamonds occur naturally in the Earth's mantle (150 km below the surface) and require time, extremely high temperatures and pressure to form into a precious gem. We are much the same, and the Threshold Guardians exist to make sure that we have the pressure on to be formed into the best versions of ourselves.

As you can probably imagine, The Threshold Guardians do not like time wasters. So many come before them with big ideas, full of wind and smoke, but so many give up at the first sign of trouble.

But once you've shown these guardians you're inspired, committed and ready to rock by buckling down and going the hard yards, ignoring naysayers who want to discourage you, thus passing the test, you are allowed safe passage into the Brave New World.

Everything is different. Once we cross the threshold, we know we can't go back, as it won't ever be the same for us. Sometimes this can present as an illusion of a brick wall and we don't know how to push past it. However, when we draw on our inner courage, we can find the way to push past the wall and move further into our new world.

It is natural to feel fear, as we are outside our comfort zones, but we can feel the fear and do it anyway. This is how courage is built.

Into your new world

It is really important when we are entering a new zone, a new world, to remember that we need to learn a different set of rules, have a different mindset, and have different rituals that support our new life. What changes do you need to implement to be able to thrive in this new world? What new tools do you need to embrace?

How do the people in your new world act differently? How do they think? What's the new 'language' they speak here?

The crossing of the threshold echoes the Acceptance of the Call with physical action, proving that the hero can follow intent with positive action.

Transition jobs are not something new to me; I have had the privilege of many different careers, all taking me closer to where I want to be. With every career change, I have learnt more about myself and the world I live in. The real threshold moment came to me in 2011 after studying Coaching and NLP (Neuro Linguistic Programming) and extended DISC profiling and really delving deeper into the human psyche. I realised I couldn't continue to train or teach in the way that I had before.

I had faced my challenges in being able to find the time to do this training and the financial resources and had taken that step across the threshold and realised that things would never be the same again for me. The way I had seen the world before had completely changed and I could only move forward and learn more and keep exploring this new world and see how that changed the way I did things. Many things changed, with two particular areas standing out:

Harness Your Hero

1. I couldn't teach stand-alone skills anymore. I had to teach in a practical, holistic and authentic way; otherwise, it just didn't feel right. This meant changing roles to find a position that was more suited to me, and this journey found me becoming the school counsellor so that I could focus on resilience and transition skills and teaching young people how to train their brains for success. Nothing else seemed that important to me if students couldn't discover how to learn in a way that worked for them to embrace lifelong learning on their terms.

2. I couldn't socialise on a regular basis with people who were not like-minded. I love spending time with people, but my time is precious, and I want my close friends to really feel the same about the world we live in as I do. This saw many of my social groups changing. It was very difficult and led me to make so many changes in my world, but I realised that I had to apply simple actions to keep on track in these demanding and trying times.

Simple action to keep us on track when we are being challenged

We all know how our lives can turn upside down with no warning, leaving us confused and doubting a positive outcome. During chaotic times, how do you stay focused on critical priorities and keep moving forward? Can you maintain focus when the world seems out of control and you see your plans disintegrate in front of you?

I recently worked with a manufacturing veteran of 25 years, who lost his job quite suddenly when the organisation changed direction. As if that unexpected transition wasn't enough, his wife told him she wanted a divorce and he found himself needing to look for somewhere else to live. In a relatively short time, his world was completely upended. He felt deflated and that everything he had worked so hard for was lost. At the time, he couldn't imagine what he could possibly do to see any light at the end of the tunnel and wondered if he would ever feel a sense of control and success in his life.

While most people do not watch their lives fall apart frame by frame as if they had stepped on to the TV screen of an episode of *Law and Order*, each of us has had to face a situation that changed the path we've been on. What can you do to keep focused when life's challenges want to pull you off course? Whether you're currently caught in a transition phase or not, the following steps are important to stay grounded.

1. Take care of your physical well-being. Are you eating, sleeping and moving your body? It is easy to let our physical wellbeing go when times get hard but, honestly, this is the worst thing we can do. Make sure you honour your body by keeping it strong and it will help you get through everything else.

2. Manage your thinking! It is easy to get caught up in what's wrong—how will you build the discipline to stop the negativity and remind yourself of the good in your life, even if it seems very small or distant at the moment?

3. Return to basics. Remember what your reasons are for getting up in the morning and what keeps you going, even on the toughest day. Do you have a clear sense of purpose in your life that expands beyond your job? If not, spending time to create this and get crystal clear on your vision can really help to stay focused.

4. Identify the top two to five people you can trust and ask for their support. How do you ensure you are getting the emotional and mental support from people you trust and who care about you?

5. If you are a person of faith, recommit yourself. What do you do that keeps you feeling spiritually connected?

By tending to these five key areas, you'll build the foundation to navigate

Harness Your Hero

the toughest of situations and come out of your challenge a stronger and more compassionate person.

My client has now embraced the challenge that was before him. He retrained and now works in aged care. He loves his new career and it has opened up doors that he never thought possible. He has bought his own home and has many hobbies and friends, and this is making him so much happier than he was, even before the time of great challenge hit. He now has a much greater appreciation for the challenges others face. He has more confidence in his abilities—and a better perspective when things get off course. As a result of his own experience, he has developed a greater humility and appreciation for others that he didn't possess before his life began to unravel. He is also better at supporting people because he has lost some of his judgmental attitude toward others. His chaos provided an opportunity for personal growth and he is one who is certainly more tenacious and more appreciative of the beauty around him.

In this busy world of ours, the mind is constantly pulled from pillar to post, scattering our thoughts and emotions, and can leave us feeling stressed, highly strung and, at times, quite anxious.

Many of us don't take five minutes to sit down and relax, let alone 30 minutes or more for a meditation session. But it is essential for our wellbeing to take a few minutes each day to cultivate mental spaciousness and achieve a positive mind–body balance.

So, if you are a busy bee like me, try using these simple mindfulness exercises to empty your mind and find some much-needed calm amidst the madness of your hectic day. When you find you are facing a Crossing of the Threshold moment (or, indeed, any of the stages of your Hero's Journey) these will be great tools to have on hand.

ACTION STEPS

Mindful breathing

This exercise can be done standing up or sitting down, and pretty much anywhere, at any time. All you have to do is be still and focus on your breath for just one minute.

Start by breathing in and out slowly. One cycle should last for approximately six seconds. Breathe in through your nose and out through your mouth, letting your breath flow effortlessly in and out of your body.

Let go of your thoughts for a minute. Let go of things you have to do later today or pending projects that need your attention. Simply let yourself be still for one minute.

Purposefully watch your breath, focusing your senses on its pathway as it enters your body and fills you with life, and then watch it work its way up and out of your mouth as its energy dissipates into the world.

If you are someone who thought they'd never be able to meditate, guess what? You are halfway there already! If you enjoyed one minute of this mind-calming exercise, why not try two or three?

Mindful observation

This exercise is simple but incredibly powerful. It is designed to connect us with the beauty of the natural environment, something that is easily missed when we are rushing around in the car or hopping on and off trains on the way to our day's activities.

Choose a natural object from within your immediate environment and focus on watching it for a minute or two. This could be a flower or an insect, or even the clouds or the stars.

Harness Your Hero

Don't do anything except really notice the thing you are looking at. Simply relax into a harmony for as long as your concentration allows. Look at it as if you are seeing it for the first time. Visually explore every aspect of its formation. Allow yourself to be consumed by its presence. Allow yourself to connect with its energy and its role and purpose in the natural world.

Mindful awareness

This exercise is designed to cultivate a heightened awareness and appreciation of simple daily tasks and the results they achieve.

Think of something that happens every day more than once; something you take for granted, like opening a door, for example. At the very moment you touch the doorknob to open the door, stop for a moment and be mindful of where you are, how you feel in that moment and where the door will lead you. Similarly, the moment you open your computer to start work, take a moment to appreciate the hands that enable this process and the brain that facilitates your understanding of how to use the computer.

These touchpoint cues don't have to be physical ones. For example, each time you think a negative thought, you might choose to take a moment to stop, label the thought as unhelpful and release the negativity. Or, perhaps each time you smell food, you take a moment to stop and appreciate how lucky you are to have good food to eat and share with your family and friends.

Choose a touchpoint that resonates with you today. Instead of going through your daily motions on autopilot, take occasional moments to stop and cultivate purposeful awareness of what you are doing and the blessings it brings your life.

Mindful listening

This exercise is designed to open your ears to sound in a non-judgmental way. So much of what we see and hear on a daily basis is influenced by our past experiences, but when we listen mindfully, we achieve a neutral, present awareness that lets us hear sound without preconception.

Select a piece of music you have never heard before. You may have something in your own collection that you have never listened to, or you might choose to turn the radio dial until something catches your ear.

Close your eyes and put on your headphones. Try not to get drawn into judging the music by its genre, title or artist name before it has begun playing. Instead, ignore any labels and neutrally allow yourself to get lost in the journey of sound for the duration of the song. Allow yourself to explore every aspect of the track. Even if the music isn't to your liking at first, let go of your dislike and give your awareness full permission to climb inside the track and dance among the sound waves.

The idea is to just listen, to become fully entwined with the composition without preconception or judgment of the genre, artist, lyrics or instrumentation.

Mindful immersion

The intention of this exercise is to cultivate contentment in the moment and escape the persistent striving we find ourselves caught up in on a daily basis. Rather than anxiously wanting to finish an everyday routine task in order to get on with doing something else, take that regular routine and fully experience it like never before.

For example, if you are cleaning your house, pay attention to every detail of the activity. Rather than treat this as a regular chore, create an entirely new experience by noticing every aspect of your actions: Feel and become the motion when sweeping the floor, sense the muscles you use when scrubbing the dishes, develop a more efficient way of wiping the windows clean. The idea is to get creative and discover new experiences within a familiar routine task.

Instead of labouring through and constantly thinking about finishing the task, become aware of every step and fully immerse yourself in the progress. Take the activity beyond a routine by aligning yourself with it physically, mentally and spiritually. Who knows, you might even enjoy the cleaning for once!

Mindful appreciation

In this last exercise, all you have to do is notice five things in your day that usually go unappreciated. These things can be objects or people—it's up to you. Use a notepad to check off five by the end of the day.

The point of this exercise is to simply give thanks and appreciate the seemingly insignificant things in life; the things that support our existence but rarely get a second thought amidst our desire for bigger and better things.

For example, electricity powers your kettle, the postman delivers your mail, your clothes provide you warmth, your nose lets you smell the flowers in the park, your ears let you hear the birds in the tree by the bus stop, but…

Do you know how these things/processes came to exist, or how they really work?

Have you ever properly acknowledged how these things benefit your life and the lives of others?

Have you ever thought about what life might be like without these things?

Have you ever stopped to notice their finer, more intricate details?

Have you ever sat down and thought about the relationships between these things and how, together, they play an interconnected role in the functioning of the earth?

Once you have identified your five things, make it your duty to find out everything you can about their creation and purpose to truly appreciate the way in which they support your life.

The cultivation of moment-by-moment awareness of our surrounding environment is a practice that helps us better cope with the difficult thoughts and feelings that cause us stress and anxiety in everyday life.

With regular practice of mindfulness exercises, rather than being led on auto-pilot by emotions influenced by negative past experiences and fears of future occurrences, we harness the ability to root the mind in the present moment and deal with life's challenges in a clear-minded, calm, assertive way.

In turn, we develop a fully conscious mind-set that frees us from the imprisonment of unhelpful, self-limiting thought patterns and enables us to be fully present to focus on positive emotions that increase compassion and understanding in ourselves and others.

Self-Reflection Questions

- The first and most important thing to decipher is: who or what are the Threshold Guardians you'll have to face in crossing the first threshold into the new world of your Hero's Journey?

- Are there people you have to meet? Places you have to go? Things you have to do that are outside of your boundary zones? Or are they fears and doubts you have to overcome inside of yourself?

- Where is your New World, and what threshold do you have to cross in order to get there? What do you have to learn in order to not just survive, but thrive in this new place?

- What are your goals? What or who do you think might be the Threshold Guardians? What resources do you have to combat the distractions and embrace the advice and learnings?

Change, like sunshine, can be a friend or a foe, a blessing or a curse, a dawn or a dusk.

William Arthur Ward

You shall judge a man by his foes as well as by his friends.

Joseph Conrad

Chapter 6:
The Road of Trials—
Allies and Adversaries

On the other side of the threshold, we find ourselves in a new environment. On this journey of discovery, we will find that we are unfamiliar with the surroundings. This can be a new hobby we are learning, new job, new home, new state or country we have moved to. It can be a new relationship or a stretch in your knowledge or financial position. It is through these trials we will meet new allies and new adversaries. You could also view these as new friends and new challenges or opposition. Through the stages of our new journey, we will meet new people and find ourselves in new situations. Self-discovery will continue to grow as well, and we will see new sides of ourselves as well as our surroundings.

Although the trials and challenges will increase, there will be friends and support also. Whenever a hero moves forward to new triumphs, they'll trigger resistance. No matter how great the vision and outcome you want to create, there will always be someone else that is not going to want that same vision and/or outcome. Sometimes it appears that the new world is more complex than you thought it was.

Resistance can be our best friend if we allow it to be. It is good when we use it to grow. In the same way our physical muscles grow by being put under pressure, we build our spiritual, mental and emotional muscles by increasing the resistance we bring to bear on them. All that we know will be brought to test in our new world; our skills, talents and abilities will all be tested.

These challenges will show us our boundary conditions very clearly and show us where we think our limits are. At this point, we will grow to climb over the hurdles and, on the occasions we don't make it, we will learn how to sharpen our tools to be able to jump our hurdles next time.

It is a good thing to bring any negative energy (thoughts) to the forefront. We can then work through what is taking that energy and harness the energy for productive purposes, thus having solved two problems with one unearthing. 1) Gained valuable energy back for moving forward, and 2) Let go of the thing that was causing us negativity.

But the more persistently you action yourself in the direction of your purpose, the more you'll attract friends and allies who'll want to support you in your cause. In these trials, as we see portrayed in so many stories, you'll meet your sidekick, your lover, your mentor, your friend, your allies and your objects of strength.

There is an expression: Condition for your position.

The more you stretch yourself, the higher the levels of your challenges become. This is to prepare you. Always face these hurdles as challenges to be overcome and with positive energy, as from these challenges will be forged your greatest resources.

You might not realise it, but the challenges you're encountering along the way are strengthening you for the biggest trial of all, as the stakes are raised and things get more and more difficult. The next threshold you're coming up against is going to be even stronger than the first Threshold Guardians. Do not be swayed.

Are you prepared for the challenges that are coming your way?

The best way that we can prepare for the trials that are coming our way, is to 1) Get to know ourselves very well, and 2) Understand what makes other people tick. When we understand what makes people do and think the way they do, it gets easier to communicate with them in a way that can bring about a win-win situation.

Introducing Behavioural Types

My form of socialising would often see me sitting around a table with friends and/or family playing cards, with some snacks served, and a beverage of some kind. One of my favourite card games is Canasta. This is a game, like many, that has an element of luck and draw of the card, but it also has to do with the strategy of how you play your cards. By looking at the cards your opponents throw out, you can start to make assumptions about what they are trying to achieve and what their next moves will be, allowing you to make decisions that will hopefully help you win the game, or at least play a strong hand.

Understanding the meaning behind people's actions and understanding their map of their world is a lot like a game of Canasta. It has been said that 90% of your success (in all areas: relationships, business, etc.) stems from your ability to effectively and accurately enter into another person's map of the world.

The reason why we do or don't get along with some people boils down to how we have (or haven't) answered two core questions that everybody is asking:

1. **Do they get me?**

The people that you are closest to, you will notice, have answered this with a solid yes and those who you relate well with, obviously, feel the same way.

2. **Are they like me?**

Once we have established a 'yes' to both of these questions, you have started to build rapport and trust with them and have a solid foundation to build on.

If we increase our ability to predict both our behaviours and that of others, we increase our ability to be more effective at creating the change that we need to create results and our personal or professional success.

Through the journey of life, there are primarily four types of people we will meet.

HOW TO RECOGNISE THE TYPE WHO WANTS TO WIN

- Is direct and says what they think
- Can appear impatient
- May talk to many people at the same time
- States own opinions as fact
- May interrupt others
- 'What is the bottom line?'
- 'How does this benefit me?'
- Often appears to be in a hurry
- Can be demanding
- May be blunt
- Very future-focused

To demonstrate an understanding of this person (answering, 'Do they get me?') simply answer their questions directly and be upfront. Sounds too simple? Most people are too busy answering their own questions and not responding directly to what is asked. This type who wants to win is interested in achieving and they seek no-nonsense, bottom-line results as a means of getting 'there'.

HOW TO ENTER INTO THEIR WORLD

- Provide alternatives
- Ensure he/she 'wins'
- Disagree only on facts
- Don't be emotional
- Enjoy the battle/debate
- Don't dominate
- Act quickly, as they decide quickly
- Be direct and specific

HOW TO COMMUNICATE WITH THEM EFFECTIVELY

- Act quickly
- Let him/her speak
- Give immediate feedback
- Stay on topic
- Focus on issues at hand
- Be direct and to the point
- Show interest
- Provide direct answers
- Acknowledge achievements

HOW TO UPSET THE TYPE WHO WANTS TO WIN

- Lose focus
- Slow down
- Take issues personally
- Be emotional
- Provide too much information
- 'Pussy-foot' around
- Go into all the details

Those who want to win are driven by the core needs of certainty and significance.
Their motto might be: 'Lead, follow or get out of the way.'
Who do you know like this?

HOW TO RECOGNISE THE TYPE WHO WANTS TO BE LIKED

- Talks a lot
- Gets easily excited
- Is open and friendly
- Is animated
- Doesn't focus much on details
- Doesn't pay close attention
- May ask the same questions several times
- Doesn't listen for long
- Jumps from subject to subject
- Stays away from hard facts
- Is open, trusting and friendly

Show them you get them by being optimistic, friendly, have fun and be okay with touch. Admire them and accept them for who they are. Indulge in a good chat and be excited about what you're talking about. Enjoy a good joke and show that you don't take life too seriously. They don't respond too well to people suffering from a strong case of 'terminal seriousness'.

HOW TO ENTER INTO THEIR WORLD

- Don't ignore them, be friendly
- Make sure you make time for a chat
- Let him/her speak
- Follow things up with them
- Chat about people and feelings
- Have fun and act silly

HOW TO COMMUNICATE WITH THEM EFFECTIVELY

- Allow them to express themselves
- Be more expressive yourself
- Be more enthusiastic
- Focus on the big picture
- Focus on the people aspects
- Help them to achieve popularity and recognition
- Create a positive atmosphere

HOW TO UPSET THE TYPE WHO WANTS TO BE LIKED

- Be too serious all the time
- Be too practical
- Set too many restrictions, they like flexibility
- Bring up negative issues
- Talk about too many details

Those who want to be liked are driven by the core needs of variety and connection.

Their motto might be: 'It's not just whether you win or lose,

it's how you look when you play the game.'

Who do you know like this?

HOW TO RECOGNISE THE TYPE
WHO WANTS TO BE COMFORTABLE

- Appears thoughtful
- New ideas and change seem to make them uncomfortable
- Appears calm
- Listens carefully
- Doesn't get easily excited
- Seems to have strong opinions but doesn't express them vocally
- Is easy-going
- Nods and goes along

Show this person you care by giving them sincere attention, patience and security. Don't change things quickly and be sure to outline all the steps before moving forward together. Knowing how things work brings them a sense of stability and comfort and so taking the time to connect with them and build certainty around something is vital.

HOW TO ENTER INTO THEIR WORLD

- Build trust
- Be sincere, don't dominate
- Secure commitment and trust bit by bit
- Present issues logically
- Don't speak quickly

HOW TO COMMUNICATE WITH THEM EFFECTIVELY

- Remember fairness and justice to all
- Provide support
- Ask specific questions to find out true needs and be patient for the answer
- Proceed in a logical order

HOW TO UPSET THE TYPE WHO WANTS TO BE COMFORTABLE

- Move too fast
- Be impatient
- Forget to provide all the detail
- Don't follow-through
- Be unreliable and inconsistent

Those who want to be comfortable are driven by the
core needs of certainty and connection.
Their motto might be: 'I don't care how much you know;
I want to know how much you care.'
Who do you know like this?

Harness Your Hero

HOW TO RECOGNISE THE TYPE
WHO WANTS TO BE RIGHT

HOW TO ENTER INTO THEIR WORLD

- Do not pressure them
- Don't talk about personal issues
- Focus on the issue at hand
- Give plenty of detailed information
- Do not touch
- Provide facts

HOW TO COMMUNICATE WITH THEM EFFECTIVELY

- Find out what their key issues are and focus on them
- Utilise written support materials
- Slow down your presentation, allowing them time to thoroughly process the info
- Answer questions calmly and carefully

HOW TO UPSET THE TYPE WHO WANTS TO BE RIGHT

- Move too fast
- Lose patience in providing all
- the requested information
- Expect decisions right away
- Spend too much time with
- small talk
- Generalise and exaggerate

Those who want to be right are driven by the core
needs of certainty and significance.

Their motto might be: 'Perfect practice makes perfect.'

Who do you know like this?

Most people mistakenly follow the golden rule verbatim:

'Treat others how you wish to be treated.'

I say mistakenly because, when you treat others as you want to be treated, you can end up offending others who have different needs, wants and expectations from you. For example, you might speak in a way that is easy for you to follow, but hard for the other person. So, here we go—the platinum rule:

'Do unto others as <u>they</u> want to be done unto.'

Remember, the type that wants to win measures their success by results; the type that wants to be liked places high value on recognition and praise; the type that wants to be comfortable places high value on sharing and trust and needs close relationships; and the type that wants to be right concerns themselves more with content than congratulations.

*There is only one corner of the universe
you can be certain of improving,
and that's your own self.*

Aldous Huxley

ACTION STEPS

You can go deep with Behavioural Profiling and if you go to our website, we can show you how. In the meantime, this little quiz will give you an introduction,

C – Concise	D – Direct
☐ Gives priority to detail & organisation	☐ Gives priority to achieving results
☐ Sets exacting standards	☐ Seeks challenges
☐ Approaches tasks and people with steadiness	☐ Approaches tasks and people with clear goals
☐ Enjoys research and analysis	☐ Is willing to confront
☐ Prefers operating within guidelines	☐ Makes decisions easily
☐ Completes tasks thoroughly	☐ Is keen to progress
☐ Focuses attention on immediate task	☐ Feels a sense of urgency
☐ Likes accuracy	☐ Acts with authority
☐ Makes decisions on a thorough basis	☐ Likes to take the lead
☐ Values standard procedures highly	☐ Enjoys solving problems
☐ Approaches work systematically	☐ Questions the status quo
☐ Likes to plan for change	☐ Takes action to bring about change
Total _____	Total _____

Harness Your Hero

S – Steadfast	I – Influence
☐ Gives priority to support others	☐ Gives priority to creating a friendly environment
☐ Enjoys assisting others	☐ Likes an informal style
☐ Approaches people and tasks with quiet and caution	☐ Approaches people and tasks with energy
☐ Has difficulty saying no	☐ Emphasises enjoying oneself
☐ Values co-operation over competition	☐ Rates creativity highly
☐ Eager to get on with others	☐ Prefers a broad approach to details
☐ Willing to show loyalty	☐ Likes participating in groups
☐ Calms excited people	☐ Creates a motivational environment
☐ Listens well/attentively	☐ Acts on impulse
☐ Prefers others to take the lead	☐ Willing to express feelings
☐ Gives priority to secure relationships and arrangements	☐ Enjoys discussing possibilities
☐ Prefers steady not sudden changes	☐ Keen to promote change
Total _____	Total _____

Self-Reflection Questions

- Is there anyone already in your life who you need to have a mentoring conversation with?

- Who are your new companions (supporters) on your new journey?

- What resources will you find to aid you?

- How will you embrace all your internal resources, such as your skills, abilities and talents and shape them to give you more leverage on your new journey?

- Who and what are the challenges and trials you're facing?

- How can you defeat them or turn them into resources for you?

- Which of these are internal challenges you have to overcome, like fear, procrastination, resistance or doubt?

You gain strength and confidence
by every experience in which you really stop
to look fear in the face.
You must do the thing you think you cannot do.

Eleanor Roosevelt

Chapter 7:
The Approach—A Time to Commit and Move to the Next Level

The Road of Trials in life, as we know, is never as easy as facing one issue and then the rest of life is a bed of roses: roses have thorns!

At this stage in our journey, we have taken a deep breath and walked right into our Innermost Cave to confront our worst fears. It is at this point that we know with certainty that there is no turning back. It is time to make it or break it, as they say.

Setbacks occur, sometimes causing the hero to try a new approach or adopt new ideas.

This is the final trial before we are able to shed off our inauthentic self and embrace our true hero. This is the part in the journey our friends and allies have been supporting us for and our challenges have been shaping us for. This is where all the past stages of our journey come together and the growth of our journey allows us to be strong enough to take the next steps.

At this point, the world can appear to go darker and life can seem bleak. It is important to remember that 'it is always darkest before the dawn'! We need these experiences for us to know when we are facing down with our 'Evil One'. Our Evil One is the ultimate challenge we face; the thing that holds us back from meeting our most desired peak.

At this point, we are looking our Evil One directly in the eye and we realise that it is a bigger and stronger adversary than we thought. It is this very moment, right here, at this point, when all hope seems lost. Our self-confidence seems to have run away from us and we can feel pinned up against the wall, with nowhere to run. Here we have found our deepest and darkest point in our Hero's Journey.

Here, we feel like no one else has ever experienced these depths before.

I feel that in these moments the gem to keep in the forefront of our minds is that we have all faced times like this. I certainly know that I have.

How about you? When was the last time you felt this way, or are you facing a similar situation in your life right now? You can choose to see it as a lonely cave, or you can choose to see it as your 'butterfly moment'. Remember that every caterpillar has to work hard to push themselves through their cocoon so that they can become the beautiful butterfly.

Many people long for personal transformation without knowing where to start to create a major change in their lives. We can often waste energy on false starts, or start in the right direction, only to find that old habits and conditioning pull us to where we were, or close to it.

What it takes to create a major shift is planning and conscious thoughtfulness. You must be aware of what your goals are and then write down how you plan to reach them. This approach is the same whether you are aiming for personal growth or a change in your relationship or career. Conscious thought is the moving force behind all changes, but it can't kick-in until you offer a direction.

Leaving a full-time, reasonably paid position to the unknown world of self-employment was definitely one of these stages for me. Not every venture that I have put my hand to has turned to gold, but I have learnt something from every opportunity that I have taken. This particular part of this journey saw me going into a very deep cave, needing to learn new skills and really reflect on myself and who I was and what I had to be able to take it to the next stage. There were some things that were keys for me to follow to get through this stage. This is an action plan for creating change.

1. **Be clear on your intention.** For a long time, I knew I wanted more out of life and I had a vague idea of what that looked like, but I wasn't really clear or focused on my intention. The question I found most useful was, 'What is it that I really want and for what purpose?' Getting my focus laser-sharp was a huge learning curve for me and really helped me to start getting the results that I was after.

2. **Go within and meditate on your intention.** Time is the greatest gift we can give ourselves. To be able to sit quietly with eyes closed and centre ourselves is not always easy in this bustling world; however, it may help to gently follow your breath for a minute or two. Visualise what you want to achieve. Don't force the images and don't fantasise. See the change you desire as clearly as you might see what your house looks like. Be realistic and calm as you see the new situation that you want to unfold. Allow yourself to feel what comes up and then look at how it serves your growth.

3. **Embrace Learning.** Read as many books as possible on the topic that you are needing to improve on. In this instance, for me, I needed to learn about running a business and also learn about human behaviour. I found myself reading about 10 books a week and listening to podcasts and watching YouTube videos and investing in training to stay focused, as most of the people from my old world thought I was stupid to do this, and I needed to find new allies and people who had experienced this part of the journey before me to learn with. This helped overcome some of the self-doubt and build my confidence in what I was doing. Implement what you are learning and take action immediately.

Harness Your Hero

4. **Let Go and deal with your Resistance.** I must admit, I was scared that I was making a mistake, even though I felt really passionate about the journey I was embarking on. One of the pieces of advice I got that really helped me was to take on board feedback. Feedback is the breakfast of champions and to take it on, reflect on it and see what pieces of gold you can take away to improve on what you are doing is awesome. There is no such thing as failure, only feedback, so sometimes we have to let go of the way we think something SHOULD be and allow it to unfold. This, too, is a place where many people falter. After seeing how much benefit they'd get from a life change, they find it too difficult to face their inner resistance. By resistance, I mean the feelings that say *no* to your intention. These can be rooted in insecurity, past failure, inertia, doubt, anxiety—the list goes on and on. I sometimes wanted to hide from the world and not get any feedback, as I didn't want to be seen as a loser or not competent. The sooner I got over that, the easier it was to come out of the cave and embrace change. But, realistically, everyone has these resistances, including the people who successfully overcome them.

5. **Understanding the landscape.** Embrace your learning style and find a way to learn that is effective and can be adopted in the shortest time frame. As daunting as it looks when you consider how much inner resistance you might have, paring it down into workable pieces is the key. Sit down and rationally plan what you need to do and what is actually feasible. I am a strong believer in gathering allies to help with any major life change. Going it alone sounds brave, but it actually isolates you and makes you vulnerable. Find someone you can trust, whether it's a confidant, spouse, mentor, or therapist. Pick someone who takes your life change as seriously as you do. Meet frequently, and share what's happening emotionally, because your emotional landscape is bound to change as you undergo any major shift.

6. **Make a plan of what is feasible.** With your ally or allies, make a list in three columns. In these columns, you are going to assess what needs to change. Column 1 is about things you can start to fix. Column 2 contains the things you have to put up with—for now. Column 3 contains the things you have to walk away from. Take your time. Go back to your lists repeatedly, until you get a clear view of your situation. Only then should you act.

7. **Achieve something positive.** Success breeds success. Start fixing the small things that you feel more confident about. Don't tackle huge personal issues in your life. Chip away at them through action you can control. It really helps to find someone who has gotten to the goal you have set for yourself. Asking someone who's been there is invaluable. Breaking your larger goals down into bite-size pieces makes them easier to swallow.

8. **Inner Success leads to outer success.** Even though you're taking action, the real change will happen in your own awareness. Walk the path as an inner path; monitor what's happening inside—a journal is a good idea here. By being self-aware, you give old habits and conditioning less of a chance to pull you backward. And if you do take a step back, note it, forgive yourself, and regroup. No matter what happens in the outside world, no one can take your inner path away from you.

9. **Connect with something bigger than yourself.** Depending on your personal beliefs, you can look to God, your soul, your higher self, your inner source—the terminology doesn't matter. What you need is a connection with whatever makes you feel trusting and safe. Only with such a connection, are major life changes achieved. For me, the path to the core of my being is through meditation, so I recommend it strongly. But it's up to you to connect with your own core, the place where desires meet fulfilment.

Harness Your Hero

10. **Review and Reward.** Don't just wait for the big goals to be done, but review how far you have come. If you have taken steps in the right direction, reward that and they we will grow.

I hope these ten steps make your life change seem realistic and reachable. Your mind, body, and spirit are designed for change. All you need is the self-confidence to know that you can set any goal that matches your highest vision. After that, the unfolding of success is a joint venture between you and yourself.

ACTION STEPS

Highlights

Reflecting on the year that has been ...

It is December 31st.
I have had the most amazing year!
Some of the successes have been:

_____

_____

_____

_____

_____

_____

_____

_____

_____

_____

_____

_____

_____

_____

_____

_____

_____

_____

_____

_____

_____

Rule of 5

Love and Relationships

1
2
3
4
5

Environment and Experiences

1
2
3
4
5

Mind and Meaning

1
2
3
4
5

Productivity and Performance

1
2
3
4
5

Wealth and Lifestyle

1
2
3
4
5

Fun and Recreation

1
2
3
4
5

Health & Vitality

1
2
3
4
5

Career and Impact

1
2
3
4
5

Harness Your Hero

Weekly Focus

	LIFE PURPOSE AREA	ACTIONS	OUTCOME WANTED	FIRST NEXT STEP	CONTACT
m					
t					
w					
t					
f					
s					
s					

Go back to your goals sheets, earlier in the book, and update.

Self-Reflection Questions

- What new language, posture, headspace, friendship groups do you need to adopt in order to survive and thrive?

- Can you see any pattern of events in your life that you feel you need to change your beliefs around?

- Do you have repeated dreams, echoes calling again and again?

- Any issues undealt with, exams unpassed? What do you need to change?

Attitude is the difference between an ordeal
and an adventure.

Bob Bitchin

Chapter 8:
Facing the Ordeal— Deep Change

Stage seven has really prepared us at this time to not avoid our allies or our challenges. In fact, it has taught us to embrace them for this stage of the journey. This is our *kahuna* moment. Here we find out what we are really made of. We stand and face our challenges and embrace our friends. We have our goals firmly in sight and we don't want to lose them.

Facing the ordeal

To overcome our greatest obstacles means going into the very depths of our darkest caves; our fears and our hidden hurts and difficulties. It is the second threshold and, as eluded to earlier, it is more difficult than the first.

In our lives, this might come as a phone call from someone you've been avoiding, an uncomfortable encounter or a more internal venture to confront your innermost fears. Here, you become aware of the negative energies that have been standing in your way, and you discover their true depth and impact.

In the Hero's Journey, we call these negative energies the 'Evil One'. In all good stories, it is the main antagonist. For us, it could be a real person, a circumstance you have to conquer, or an internal obstacle.

So, of the three types of Evil One, which has taken you to your innermost cave? Is there a person that comes to mind who you need to face, rather than avoid? Or perhaps it is a situation you are avoiding? Limiting beliefs are our third cave. Is there a limiting belief that is holding you down or spinning you round?

What is the one thing that is most stopping you from reaching your 'treasure' right now?

It's your move!

Harness Your Hero

ACTION STEPS

To be able to face your fears head-on and to be able to turn challenges into opportunities, we must identify and remove our self-limiting beliefs. Let's look at a process for achieving this.

Identify Your Limiting Beliefs

In your playbook, write down all the limiting beliefs you have regarding your life, your goals and your ability to be able to achieve them.

When I was first posed with the question of discovering my limiting beliefs, I really didn't know where to start.

Then it was posed to me that I should write down what my ideals would be in each area of my life (we have looked at these areas several times now). Write down or look back on what your goals are. And then ask yourself the question, 'Why haven't I achieved it yet?' Really think about this and write down everything that comes to mind. These are your limiting beliefs!

For instance, when I had a health goal to exercise for one hour a day, I couldn't seem to achieve this, no matter what I did. I applied the above exercise to this goal.

I came up with:

- Didn't have an hour a day.

- Too tired to exercise.

- Didn't have the right equipment or space.

- Didn't have enough money.

- Hurt too much.

So, these were my limiting beliefs around exercise. Now, that doesn't mean to say that there wasn't something in each of these statements, but what I needed to do was turn each of these into a positive.

The brain is an interesting thing and what we tell ourselves, it will expand and create a belief. It looks for clues to back up what we believe. We need to get the brain looking for clues that highlight success.

I started looking for times that proved these limiting beliefs wrong. Well, if I had time to go to work and to have a shower and do all the other things I had to do, there was time to exercise, and I came up with several examples where I had made the time to exercise.

I often was tired, but I looked at times when I had gone to bed early and got up early and started the day with a walk, etc. and how good it had felt.

I wrote down the times that I had exercised without fancy equipment or needing to buy a gym membership.

A-ha moments! I could turn each of these around if I wanted to. So, then it was about, 'Why are these beliefs not serving me?' Well, they were stopping me from getting healthier and having more energy.

Where did this belief come from? Interestingly, I had tried to do gym with friends of mine and walk with friends of mine and I just couldn't keep up and was left completely wrecked, tired and sore for weeks! I was embarrassed and lost confidence and wanted to avoid the pain!

Ah! I needed to reframe the situation: If I do shorter timed sessions, more frequently throughout the day, I will gain more energy and start to feel better. I found that I loved to dance and I found a program called Body Groove. That, with Pilates,

Harness Your Hero

became my new game plan in getting fitter and healthier. It was about finding the right fit for me and not trying to fit into someone else's routine.

1. Now, in your playbook, I would like you to mind-map all your limiting beliefs. Really take the time to identify the thinking that is holding you back. Work through each area of life in the format that I have described and draw out the limiting beliefs.

2. On the template on the next page, I would like you to work through each of the stages I discussed that I worked through.

3. With the reframe, write down a new belief that will overwrite your limiting belief that is true for you.

What this does is let you know that there are flaws in your belief.

When going about your day, actively look for flaws in your limiting beliefs. You can try identifying situations or people that have combated the same limiting beliefs that you are currently facing and look at how they overcame them. Thanks to Google, there are many examples we can easily access.

My favourite example of beating your limiting beliefs

The best example of limiting beliefs and proving them wrong is the story of Roger Bannister and the four-minute mile.

It was said to be 'fact' that it was absolutely impossible for a person to run a mile in under four minutes. Runners and athletes from all over the world were trying to do it and no one had been able to. It was deemed impossible. It became a shared limiting belief, except for one man—Roger Bannister.

Roger would visualise himself running the mile in under four minutes (oh, the power of visualisation). He would do this so often that there were moments he would feel he had already done it.

Roger did break the four-minute barrier, and the most exciting part about this story is, once the belief was broken, 26 other athletes were able to break it the following year!

As you work through this activity, emotions can arise. This is okay. Just allow yourself space and time to work through it. Emotions can be a huge catalyst for change.

By gaining a clear understanding of where these beliefs are hindering your life and the consequences they are having, it will help in creating the driving need for you to make the change.

Visualise the change

The last part of the process is to visualise the change in your own life.

Visualisation is one of the most effective ways of changing your thoughts and getting your mind focused on what really matters in your life. It is one of the most effective ways of creating success in your life.

Take the time now to close your eyes and picture yourself performing your new belief. Feel the experience and feel the emotions. Let your new belief sink into your consciousness.

Spend time doing this for each of your beliefs

Once you have completed these steps, read over your old limiting beliefs. Do they still ring true for you?

Give yourself some time. Repeat this process if need be. The key is identifying situations where you yourself have proved the belief no longer true for you, as well as where others have proven this wrong.

By reframing the belief into a positive one and visualising yourself living with your new belief, you will start to notice the decisions you make in your life are more aligned with what you want to do and where you want to go.

Self-Reflection Questions

Let's review dysfunctional behaviours, limiting beliefs or self-sabotage. These things will really get in the way during this stage.

- What or who is your 'Evil One'?

- What do you fear the most in life? How can you turn this fear around into a strength?

- Is it your past? Failure or success?

- Whom do you need to confront?

- If you do not deal with it, that fear will come upon you, because it must be faced. hat are the first steps moving forward?

No person was ever honoured for what he received. Honour has been the reward for what he gave.

Calvin Coolidge

Faith is to believe what you do not see; the reward of this faith is to see what you believe.

Saint Augustine

Chapter 9:
Receiving Your Reward

Throughout the last eight stages of our personal Hero's Journey, there has been a lot of work and challenges to be faced. This needs to be rewarded with some breathing room— being able to stop and smell the roses and just bask in the successes of the moment.

This is a big step. We have got into the rink with our Evil One and won. We have moved into an authentic state with ourselves and know that we need to be true to what is important to us. At this point, we have survived the fire and stepped up to be our true hero. It doesn't matter how small we tell ourselves the challenge we have overcome was or the success we have reached is, the fact of the matter is, we did it! Don't let this go without giving it its due reward. Often the reward is there. The question is, are we receiving it?

We have survived the trials and 'death' of whatever we had to let go of to achieve the reward. We are forever changed through this transformation.

In school, if we pass a test, we get the reward of a good grade. In life, we receive rewards as well. Often the tests are harder and we haven't been able to study for them! The ordeal we have gone through is not the end of our story. In fact, it is the middle of our story! We go through these difficult challenges so that we can obtain the thing we so desperately desire.

This is the point we have been working towards; it is time to step up and claim our 'treasure'. This is the most important outcome of our Hero's Journey.

The outcome could be many things. You may have completed training or gained your ideal employment. You may have started in an ideal relationship, or gained the finances you need to purchase something you have wanted. Or possibly you

Harness Your Hero

have secured something less tangible, but equally important, like gained confidence, knowledge or self-worth. In many stories, we hear of the treasure being called the 'reward' or the 'elixir': something that, once you have, will create change that will have a lasting impact. This is the opportunity to have a much-deserved break from the relentless pace of the journey. Taking these breaks is as important as any other part of our quest. Never underestimate this step in your journey.

How do you unwind and celebrate? For me, I love going to the zoo or spending time with animals or being near water. I also love music and spending time with my husband. I will give myself the gift of time as a reward. I once heard someone talk about 'dating yourself' and thought this was a great idea. Making time for you in your diary is really important and maybe weekly or fortnightly or even monthly, you put a celebration date in the diary to reflect and celebrate all that you have achieved.

Now think about what are the best ways for you to relax and celebrate your journey?

Even before we hold the reward, we have already started a transformation from the journey. We have had the trials and tests that have helped us forge into our new world and given us the challenges to grow. We have faced the weaknesses within us, and embraced the strengths and resources, as well. We have assessed who our allies are, and are not. The journey itself has already given us many gifts, rewards and experiences to enhance our lives.

We've all had times when we've been victorious over the challenges of life and achieved our greatest desires. Times like that, when we feel on top of the mountain, let us know just how confident and resourceful we truly can be.

Celebrating each and every one of these victories helps us stack up our self-esteem and confidence, and that is worth investing in, no matter how small the achievement. Keeping a gratitude journal of three things each day that are blessings to you is a great way to get into a habit that will support your celebrating these victories, and also keep you 'locked on' to your positive resources.

I often take for granted the rewards and stay focused on the challenge. Often, we are on many Hero's Journeys simultaneously and it can be hard to focus on all that is going on. At one stage in my life, my financial journey was just starting a new beginning with changes needed as the pain caused me to answer the Call to Adventure and start a new career that had the potential for better dividends. At the very same time, a new relationship with my now-husband was at its 'Crossing the Threshold' moment and, with some health breakthroughs that also occurred around that same time, there was a reward for me to receive. I felt so overwhelmed by the other 'journeys' I was on, that I nearly overlooked these really important and positive stages of my transformation.

It is in the receiving and embracing of the rewards that we work out that we are stronger and more powerful than we ever imagined, and, in those moments, we realise we have the strength to apply those strategies to other areas of our lives.

Never underestimate the power of celebration and acknowledgement of all the rewards, big and small, in your world.

The reward stage of the Hero's Journey allows the hero, and those sharing the journey, a temporary reprieve from the relentless pace. The reward phase of the story can serve numerous purposes.

Celebration

Surviving the challenges and seizing a prize is a major achievement. This definitely sounds like a celebration moment to me! This can be a real rite of passage and allowing the positive emotions to flow through us and rev it up with some celebration time is a must and a great use of this stage of the journey.

Recap and reflection

Campfire moments (literal or metaphorical) are really important. This can happen in nature or a five-star restaurant. It is a time to bring together all of those who have been a part of this particular journey and recap. Reflect and refocus. You could recap your experiences so far, perhaps giving some important insight into what the events meant to you. This could also be used to review what is important as you prepare for the next stages of your journey and what you want to take with you.

New knowledge

Surviving challenges can change how you perceive things. You very well may have gained new insights.

They say knowledge is power, so your superpowers may have grown to:

- See through characters' behaviours and see their intentions (highlighting areas you had been blind to, etc.).

- Realise your true destiny and/or heritage.

- Have a moment of clarity to see new paths for your quest.

What other superpowers could you have developed?

The long and short of it

The reward stage is about action. The hero (that is you) must seize this moment. We must take the elixir, draw the magic sword, take hold of love, embrace our destiny or all of the above. We have spent much time reacting and doubting. Through conquering the ordeal, we have earned this moment to take the action we have desired since answering the call.

Self-Reflection Questions

- When was the last time you claimed your reward?

- How did it feel?

- What empowering beliefs did you build, or can you build, from that experience to support you moving forward?

- How many more victories can you remember, right now?

- When did you last reward yourself for change made, and victory accomplished?

The more you praise and celebrate your life,
the more there is in life to celebrate.

Oprah Winfrey

Transformation literally means
going beyond your form.

Wayne Dyer

Ordinary people who are just kind of just
going about their lives are transformed into
heroes because they have the courage

to put their voices out there.

Viola Davis

Chapter 10:
The Hero is Transformed—A New Life

Wasn't it great to take some time to celebrate? Rewards are important to support growth and give you a well-earnt rest. However, ultimately, rewards are rest and reflection stops on a continual journey. We are not meant to stop growing. Like I said in an earlier chapter, we are either green and growing or red and rotting. Thus, progress in life is truly about reinvention.

There is a difference between reinvention and reward. Basically, seeking a reward usually implies an 'end'. You win the trophy and then you're 'done'. That's not what you want to aim for long-term. As stated in the previous chapter, looking out for the 'rewards' of your journey and celebrating the successes and the goals reached is very important, as is the next stage. As soon as you say you're 'done', you are no longer reaching and stretching yourself, which means you stop growing.

Reinvention is what allows you endless opportunities to continue exploring new parts of yourself. This is what takes you from endless striving to creating a better version of you that grows and experiences life on a whole new level.

There are a few things to keep in mind to do this.

1. See yourself from outside of yourself.

Imagine you are a sculptor.

A sculptor looks at raw material in front of them and endlessly contemplates new ways to shape it. If they think of something to change, there is no emotional attachment.

They just do it.

This is how we need to see ourselves—as a work of art, always in progress. No need to get upset or come down hard on yourself when you see something you do not like. Instead, like the sculptor, just get to work on moulding yourself into a more ideal you.

2. Find the habit associated with the thing you want to change.

Far too often, we can focus too much on the thing we want to change instead of the habits that formed the thing in the first place. For example, someone who is trying to solve being overweight with doing a lot of ab exercises, might not have acknowledged that there are problems with nutrition and sleep.

To truly reinvent aspects of yourself, you have to find the habit that created that trait in the first place—and then adjust the habit.

3. Practise every day, no matter what.

Change is not something you do some days and then take a break from other days. Change requires a shift in lifestyle.

It requires daily dedication, to the point where that new habit takes the place of an old one and no longer requires conscious effort.

4. Set realistic goals.

You can't just wake up one morning and say, 'I'm not going to be impatient anymore!' Chances are: yes, you are.

And you actually help yourself by acknowledging that a bad habit like that won't be solved immediately. Instead, set the goal to be more patient during your team meeting that happens each week. Use that as an isolated practice space and subconscious reminder of what it is you want to practise.

Focus on that for a few weeks, and then go from there.

5. Constantly look in the mirror.

Things get dangerous when you refuse to stop and really look at yourself—when you avoid self-reflection.

There is a time and a place for 'go, go, go' mode, and then there is a time and place for reflection mode.

Both are necessary.

And you will quickly find that unless you take the time to ask yourself the tough questions, you will fall off track and not know how you got there.

6. Surround yourself with people who will tell you the truth.

If everyone around you is telling you 'yes', then you have a serious problem.

You need people who are going to challenge and question you. You need people who won't be afraid to tell you the truth.

Tough feedback is essential for personal growth.

7. You have to take risks.

You will never become the person you want to be by continuing to be the person you currently are. Growth's only request is that you step out of your comfort zone. That's it. And unless you are willing to take that risk, to take that uncomfortable leap into the unknown, you will forever stay exactly where you are.

Reinvention is an art; it is a process. It is not a 'quick fix' or an 'overnight

Harness Your Hero

solution'. It is a deliberate practice, day in and day out, until you realise who it is you want to be, you already were all along.

This is a fundamental point of your Hero's Journey. At this time, you have proven that, despite the very real danger of failure, and despite facing your worst demons and fears, you have chosen to see through your Hero's Journey until you reach out and grab the outcome you desire. Now you know that you have the strength to do it and so much more.

Being very clear on your 'why' is crucial for knowing what the greater cause is for which you're willing to overcome your limitations or challenges and push on through. What are the resources you'll need that will help you do that most effectively?

The Climax.

This is the moment; your 'blaze of glory' moment to take up your resources and become an even better version of you.

At this moment, the things you thought impossible can soon prove the theory...

IM – POSSIBLE.

You can achieve what appeared to be the impossible.

Make sure you celebrate each of these moments: it could be an argument you got resolution in, a decision you were able to finally make, or a deal secured. You might have done some internal work. It might be a rule you had for your life that you have changed, or a rule made. It might be a limiting belief you finally have broken through, or that treasured moment of hard-earned clarity you gained about your own life.

At this point, you are the master of your negative energies. You have developed and sculpted yourself so far beyond your ordinary world that you no longer have anything within you that can take you back to your ordinary world.

At this point, you are a true hero.

ACTION STEPS

Think about the areas of your life that you want something different in. It might be good to reflect back on your Wheel of Life. Then review the steps for the transformation.

Who You Were	**Who you currently are**	*Who you want to be*
Example: My personal image. I went through a gothic stage; very dark colours and wanted to try and present myself as tough and then tried the hippy look and then, as I started work, went for the suit and high business look.	Jeans and flowing top is my current look. I don't feel like my image really reflects the image I want to present. Need to think about what that is.	I want to feel (and look) vibrant, energetic and switched on. A go get 'em gal. I like classic black and gold and also really want to be able to rock funky colour.

Have this list in mind when you are thinking about your self-reflection questions.

Harness Your Hero

Self-Reflection Questions

- What part of your masterpiece do you want to 'upgrade'?

- What habits need reviewing in order to get to the next best version of you?

- What risks are begging you to give them a go?

- Who can support your 'accountability' with this next step?

There's no place like home.

Dorothy in the *Wizard of Oz*

The whole journey is just about coming home.

Sean Gobin

Chapter 11:
Hero Returns Home

It has been a brave journey and you have claimed your reward. All that is left at this point is to return to your ordinary world. Bring what you know into your world. Learn to contextualise to expand their world and ours.

Shift the tide. Your World Transforms…

On return to your ordinary world, it is evident that you are not the person you were when you left. You've been strengthened and shaped and moulded by your journey. The New World is now a terrain you know well and have positive experiences with. You are now a dual citizen, able to live in the old world and live within the new. You bring what you have learnt into your world.

When I was looking at going overseas for the first time, I certainly felt like the 'new world' was unknown. I was a little nervous and not sure what to expect. But the more we ventured, the more comfortable I became, and that form of travelling is now something that I have done again and feel very comfortable with.

Using your rewards

After all of the self-reflection and self-growth, we realise there has to be something more. The journey home is when we start to think about how to pass on what we have learnt; how we can contribute to something beyond ourselves. We are returning with our treasure. What if we can share it so that it benefits more than just us? How can we use it to help improve the people living around us in the Ordinary World?

In the same way that we didn't know what lay beyond our world until we went on our journey, many others have no idea what lies outside of it either and what can be possible for them if they just step outside of their comfort zones and cross the threshold into the new world.

From your journey, you have returned with tales of your experiences. This may be the Call of Adventure for others. Some may be scared if they know the sacrifices and challenges you faced and that may be enough to put them off. What if you can share with them that those sacrifices and challenges were the making of you and could be the making of them. Let them know you didn't have all the answers in the beginning, but the trick was starting the journey and then working out how to succeed at it and gain your reward.

This may be your opportunity to see someone else start their own Hero's Journey. You may, in fact, change roles and become the wise mentor, as someone was to you before.

Sharing is caring!

The truth that you can be certain of is that the treasures you've accumulated in your life, whether intangible like knowledge, or tangible like money, will (if you allow it to) benefit someone else out there who needs it. This then begs the question, what circumstances or to what people can you offer the benefits of your rewards? What can you contribute, how can you contribute and to whom?

Self-Reflection Questions

- What 'elixirs' do you have now to pass on to others?

- Who do you know that you can pass these on to?

- How can you share your legacy?

- What new rituals must you embrace to maintain your new state?

What makes you a hero is not your triumph over adversity but your ability to transform the minds and hearts of others as a result.

Marcia Reynolds

Follow your bliss and the universe will open doors for you where there were only walls.

Joseph Campbell

Chapter 12:
The Next Hero's Journey

Having experienced the stages of the Hero's Journey and finding your way home with your prize, you may have found comfort in the old; celebrating with friend and family and taking some well-earnt down-time. However, you may have found that after settling back down into things, you again get that niggling feeling that you have had before that something isn't quite right. You realise that you are after something more.

Dr Clare W. Graves, physiologist and creator of Spiral Dynamics, wrote:

The Never-Ending Quest

At each stage of human existence, the adult man is off on his quest of his holy grail, the way of life he seeks by which to live. At his first level he is on a quest for automatic physiological satisfaction. At the second level he seeks a safe mode of living, and this is followed in turn, by a search for heroic status, for power and glory, by a search for ultimate peace; a search for material pleasure, a search for affectionate relations, a search for respect of self, and a search for peace in an incomprehensible world. And, when he finds he will not find that peace, he will be off on his ninth level quest. As he sets off on each quest, he believes he will find the answer to his existence. Yet, much to his surprise and much to his dismay, he finds at every stage that the solution to existence is not the solution he has come to find. Every stage he reaches leaves him disconcerted and perplexed. It is simply that as he solves one set of human problems he finds a new set in their place. The quest he finds is never-ending.

Life, at its very essence, is a series of journeys. Thus, we know our journey does not end with our one journey. In fact, sometimes we are on many Hero's Journeys simultaneously.

In life, we are either green and growing or red and rotting and, let's face it, our life's quest is to grow. We want to become ever more mature in the person we are, seeking new treasures, new challenges, new allies and experiencing more and more new worlds. Each day, moving forward, we keep growing our skills and abilities to become more of the hero we want and need in our lives.

So, one day, you set out on a new Hero's Journey, and the adventure begins again.

Once you find yourself at the end of a Hero's Journeys, what is the next adventure you can begin? What is one new goal you can put into action that will excite you, stretch and grow you?

In looking to answer this question, I decided it was time to update my bucket list. It felt good to see that I could tick a few things off my list and add some things to it as well.

Every man dies—not every man really lives.

William Ross

The only people who fear death are those with regrets.

Author Unknown

What's A Bucket List?

If you haven't heard about the term 'bucket list', it is a list of all the things you want to achieve, dreams you want to fulfil and life experiences you desire to experience while on this planet.

Why Create A Bucket List?

If you don't live your days by personal goals and plans, chances are you spend most of your time caught up in a 'take it how it flows' kind of life. This is okay, if it is flowing in a way that works, but how do you even know that if you don't know where you would like to 'flow' to?

Ever felt that your days are passing you by without any meaningful outcomes to speak of? What did you accomplish in the past three months? What are your upcoming goals for the next three months? Look at the things you did and the things you're planning to do next: would they mean anything to you if you were to leave this earth today? Having a bucket list reminds you of what's really important so you can act on these things.

Even if you frequently live by goals or to-do lists, they are probably framed within a certain context, e.g. performance, career, health. (We have looked at goals in many aspects of this book.) A bucket list opens up the context. It's a forum to set down anything and everything you've ever wanted to do, whether it's big, small or random.

It's just like planning ahead all the highlights you want for YOUR whole life.

Even though goal setting is already my number one go-to, I still found many new things to do while I was writing and editing my own list.

It was an incredibly insightful exercise. What's more, coming up with my list gave me a whole new layer of enthusiasm knowing what's in store ahead!

The whole point of creating a list is to maximise every moment of our existence and live our life to the fullest. It's a reminder of all the things we want to achieve in our time here, so that instead of wasting our time in pointless activities, we are directing it fully toward what matters to us.

It can help us to decide on which is the next all-important Hero's Journey to embark on.

Create Your Bucket List

If you don't have a bucket list, I highly recommend you create one. How much will it cost? Zero. How long will it take? Probably 30 minutes to an hour, or more if you get really caught up in the writing. What do you stand to gain? Significant clarity and focus on what you want from your life. It's an invaluable exchange.

If you already have your list, take this opportunity to review it. See if there are new items you want to add-on. If so, add them in. Check if all the items listed are still relevant. If not, remove them.

Now, take out your pen and paper or open up a text document. Start writing down what comes to mind as you read these questions:

- What if you were to die tomorrow? What would you wish you could do before you die?

- What would you do if you had unlimited time, money and resources?

- What have you always wanted to do but have not done yet?

- Are there any countries, places or locations you want to visit?

- What are your biggest goals and dreams?

- What do you want to see in person?

- What achievements do you want to have?

- What experiences do you want to have/feel?

- Are there any special moments you want to witness?

- What activities or skills do you want to learn or try out?

- What are the most important things you can ever do?

- What would you like to say/do together with other people? People you love? Family? Friends?

- Are there any specific people you want to meet in person?

- What do you want to achieve in the different areas of life? (Look at the Wheel of Life for an idea on areas.)

- What do you need to do to lead a life of the greatest meaning?

Come up with as many items as you can. The items should be things you have not done yet. Don't stop until you have listed at least 101 things! If you find yourself stuck, chances are you are mentally limiting/constraining yourself. Release those shackles —your bucket list is meant to be a list of everything you want to achieve, do, see, feel and experience in your life.

In Conclusion

You now have a tool that is a wonderful reflection of the different stages in our lives, and a great compass to support us on our own journeys. As we set out on our new journey, it is good to be open and looking for who might be our wise mentors. What or who might be our Threshold Guardians that are putting us to the test?

When we face our challenges, we need to be looking for resources and identifying our allies. When we feel that we have our back against the wall, sometimes the best thing to do is take the next positive step.

Just as your life can be a Hero's Journey, so can it also be full of many different yet simultaneous Hero's Journeys overlapping at the same time. You could be in a different point in your journey at work, compared to your journey in your home life, with a new skill or ability you are honing, or a business you're getting up off the ground.

Self-Reflection Questions

- What new mentoring do you need as a result of your new status? What new resources do you need?

- What internal keys need to unlock external doors?

- To whom will you impart your new-found knowledge and experience?

- Who will you mentor on their journey? Who can you coach?

- What is your next adventure? Where is the next mountain?

- As you read through these chapters on the Hero's Journey, were there any that struck you more than others? How did it help you better understand where you are on your current journey? And how could you use the secrets that have been revealed to make your journey even smoother?

In reading through this book, you have embarked on a Hero's Journey. I hope it has shaped you and given you an elixir to take back to your Ordinary World and help shape your next adventure.

Onwards and upwards to your next Hero's Journey.

We would like to invite you on your next Hero's Journey.

Would you like to get more including one to one personalised

attention to support you in taking life to the next level?

Readers Introductory Offer

'Your Personal Success Planning Session'

Reserve your one-to-one 30-minute spot
with the Author of *Harness Your Hero*
to pull back the curtain of YOUR Hero's Journey
and experience a vitalising, inspiring and productive
conversation around what the next level of your life
looks like for you.

Contact our specialised team today to find out how
we can make your dreams a reality.

https://www.harnessyourhero.com/introductoryoffer

Training & Coaching

Phone: +61 8 8120 0255
Email: ask_us@infusecentral.com
www.infusecentral.com

PERSONAL NOTE

We understand that we are working with busy, effective and real human beings, not robots. With this in mind, we are flexible in working with you to develop a program, presentation and/or coaching package that meets your requirements. At any point along the journey, we are open to any request and happy to discuss any queries that you may have.

What are you waiting for?
Are you waiting for someone to take out the risk
and create a win-win situation for you?
You are the most important part of our business,
and we like to prove it:

Our 100% Satisfaction Guarantee

Our number one goal is to exceed the value you expect from our training programmes and coaching packages. If you are not completely satisfied with the training or coaching provided, we will refund 100% of the training/coaching cost and let you keep the workbooks and handouts. You could say that our guarantee is 150% because it far exceeds a mere 100% return. Whatever we call it, you win! We want to reassure you that you are getting the best possible value for your training/coaching investment and take away any risk. What more could you ask for? Great value with no risk. Why not give us a call today?